PREPAREDNESS

The Basics and Beyond

By

Mark A. Smith

STAY SAFE

MA Smith

Auctoritas

Cover Art designed by Justin Evangelista © 2012

PREPAREDNESS: THE BASICS AND BEYOND
© 2012 BY MARK SMITH

The information provided in this book is the product of the author's experience. That doesn't mean it's going to work the same way for you. Use your common sense. Neither the author nor the publisher will accept responsibility for problems arising from your decisions or your actions or inactions.

ISBN-10: 0985801743

ISBN-13:978-0-9858017-4-8

AUCTORITAS PUBLISHING LLC
848 S. Kimbrough
Springfield, MO 65806

DEDICATION

*To my son Lane who is the best part of
me*

*To the 343 New York City firefighters
who lost their lives on 9/11.
Rest well my brothers*

CONTENTS

Preface
A FEW THOUGHTS ON PREPAREDNESS...

The timing of this book is a reflection on world events. I believe the need for self-reliance has never been higher. Worldwide events of the last decade have demonstrated this all too well. Riots, wars, terror attacks, droughts, food shortages, economic upheavals and more have all played across our television screens with frightening regularly. Even our own government through the use of Public Service Announcements (PSA) has been urging the population to have a stockpile of food and water on-hand stating that they cannot provide for everyone following an emergency.

PSA's, coming from FEMA, the Federal Emergency Management Agency, started out by saying people should have three days worth of food and water on-hand. The most recent PSA I saw stated that amount recommended is a week minimum. Not enough, in my opinion, but at least it is something. Ten years ago the government said little to nothing about being self reliant so this is a step in the right direction. A small step but anything at this point is a good thing. Civil defense in this country is woefully under-funded and largely ignored, unlike in decades past.

What is going on in this country regarding preparedness leaves a good deal to be desired and then some. This is especially true when you compare what some countries are actively doing to better protect their citizens. For instance in Israel ALL new homes must be constructed with an internal "safe" room. This is a hardened room designed to protect the occupants from attacks such as the

Searchers comb the wreckage of what had been a 2-story apartment complex after the Joplin, Missouri, EF-5 tornado in 2011. The wreckage was 3 to 4 feet deep in some areas. The effect was as if the city had been dropped into a giant blender. No one expected a storm this bad.

massive rocket shelling of northern Israel by Hezbollah
forces in 2006. Now I understand fully that the United States
doesn't face all the immediate threats that Israeli citizens do
but I feel the comparison is a valid one. Imagine requiring
homebuilders here to do the same!

Some people are reluctant to admit that they and their
family could become affected by anything that could disrupt
their existence. I believe this is due to the reasoning that if
they acknowledge that a potential problem exists, then at
some point they will have to do something to address it.
"Ignorance is bliss" is another, less polite way of saying this.
The reality is that all too often people tend to think only "big
picture" regarding an event that would force them into a
survival situation. Since the likelihood of that happening is
slim, why worry?

For them this means only a war, or some other
nation-wide crisis but it is far more likely that what affects
them will be regional or just local in scale. An ice storm, a
flood, and a big one today is the loss of a job. I can speak
from personal experience on that topic.

I was out of work awhile back due to some serious
injuries I suffered. It was our extended stock of on-hand
food, dry goods and paper goods that helped us through.
This period lasted several months, and it was financially
trying to be sure. When you only have to worry about
having to buy the bare essentials such as bread, milk, and
eggs, it stretches what money you have a great deal farther.
Once I was able to return to work we rebuilt our stocks as
rapidly as we could. We had made it through a difficult

time, thanks in no small part to our commitment to being more self reliant. We certainly weren't eating steak and lobster but we never went hungry, and there was a great deal of variety in our diet.

So, ready to talk some about planning? Then read on and let's get started!

SURVIVAL QUIZ

Please look over and then answer the following questions which should better help you to understand what it is that you are preparing for.

- Does the area I live in experience severe weather on at least a yearly basis? (Hurricanes, tornadoes, floods, blizzards, heat waves, etc.)

- Does the area I live in experience earthquakes? If so how often and usually how severe?

- Is the area I live in subject to volcanic activity?

- Is the area I live in within three miles of the coast or other major body of surface water?

- Do I have more or less than one week of food and water on-hand right now? (Foods you can prepare without electricity or natural gas)

- Do I have the ability to obtain clean, drinkable water if I have none at my residence?

- What do I feel is the greatest threat to my long term survival? (Terrorist incident, economic issues, severe weather, etc)

- How many people am I *realistically* planning to prepare to care for in case of an event? (This number may be larger than you think)

- What, if any, are the special health concerns I will have to deal with post event? (Diabetes, high blood pressure, disabilities, elderly, etc.)

- What is the likely length of the event I am most realistically planning for?

- Is there a military base, government building or other high value target within three miles of my residence or place of work?

- What, if any, crisis situations (floods, earthquakes, robberies, etc) have you been through in the past? What did you learn from that experience?

- What is my level of comfort with being prepared?

Once you have completed this checklist you should have a much more defined idea of what it is that you feel the threats and concerns you have are. You can't make any informed decisions regarding your plans without the proper information.

NOTES

NOTES

1
PREPAREDNESS ON A BUDGET

Okay, so you want to increase your level of preparedness to better ensure the health and safety of your family. Great! Good for you. The reason or reasons for this decision aren't all that important, but the choice is the right one, believe that. You are, however, concerned though that it will cost a fortune. "Oh, I think I need this, I heard I need that, maybe I should have three of those, etc…" There is a huge amount of far less-than-great information floating around out there. I am going to help steer you clear of as much of that as I can.

Don't despair; prepping (a slang term for preparedness) isn't nearly as hard as it seems. Honest. I make my living as a preparedness consultant and have helped many people over the years, a number of whom were just beginning in the lifestyle.

When I was married, my wife and I averaged less

than $40,000 in combined income nearly every year that we were married (12 years). Despite that we still managed to accumulate much of the good, equipment and training that is discussed in this book. We simply made prepping a priority and adjusted our lifestyle accordingly. We raised our three children, enjoyed vacations, meals out, and a life style we were comfortable with, all the while adding to our preps and training. The same is true of when we went shooting; it was a fun family activity that teaches weapon safety, marksmanship and responsibility. In fact many of our family camping trips were a combination of training for survival and fun family time.

It is vital to remember that preparedness is a lifestyle -- not a fad, not a hobby, not a stage to go through. If you are going to do this -- and you have bought this book so you are thinking hard about it -- then to commit to doing it. Am I finished with my own purchases? Not even! There is always something else to add, one more can of something, another thing to learn. Despite what it sounds like it is not a bottomless money pit. I warn you that it might seem like it at times, but in the long run what is staying alive worth to you?

Something to always remember: it is YOU who is ultimately responsible for your own well being and that of your family. It is NOT the government in whatever form, federal, state, city, whatever, not a relief organization, not a church or other faith based group, YOU...I know that goes against what we are bombarded with via the media and other sources. It is up to you to take care of you.

Following Katrina is was as many as SIX days before

anyone arrived in some areas just to begin to assess the needs of the area. Not to begin to provide aid, just to assess what was needed so they could then arrange for it to be brought to the area. Could you survive six days without food, fresh water, shelter, heat, hygiene? Could you? Possibly, but it wouldn't be pleasant at all.

Meat shelves stripped bare during an ice storm, Missouri 2007.

Can those agencies and groups I mentioned above help? Sure they can. It is true that some of these people will help after the fact and in some cases, for a long time after the fact. But what about the first hour, the first day…it could take outside assistance quite some time to reach you and your family, especially if the event is a large scale regional one like a hurricane or earthquake. The initial help you need is likely only going to come from one place -- you.

Simple and straightforward as that. I cannot put it any plainer.

One of the hardest aspects of this is understanding that many people in this country routinely live beyond their means. Eating out much too often, buying new cars when there is nothing wrong with the vehicle(s) they currently have, wanting to add this or that to the house just because they can, taking expensive vacations when a modest vacation does the same thing. The cost of two nights dining out for a family of four could pay for a big chunk of groceries or paying extra on a credit card. The kids want all name brand clothes, fine, have them go get a job and let them pay for it themselves. I'm not kidding. It will teach them the power of work and appreciation for what they have.

The key to survival spending is SMART spending. I would absolutely **not** recommend that you rush out and get a second or third mortgage on the house and then spend it all on supplies and equipment. Preparedness is about the LONG TERM. It isn't just surviving to live, it is surviving to thrive! Remember, the basics of what you need to survive are food, water, heat and shelter. If you have these things then you can better tackle whatever comes next.

The other side of the prepping coin so to speak is being realistic. Just because you have food, water, shelter and such doesn't mean all your problems are magically solved. There could still be environmental issues to deal with, criminal activity, weather, government heavy-handedness and more.

-o-

Some smart spending tips to get you started on preparing for long term survival.

A) **Start with the basics,** food, water and the means to cook them without grid power. Each time you go and buy your regular groceries you add a couple of items above and beyond what you normally purchase. Food items like four extra cans of vegetables, two more packages of pasta, one extra box of rice, five more pounds of sugar. If you do something similar to this each time you go shopping in no time you have added a full week's worth of food to add to your on-hand stock. Then it becomes two weeks, then a month and so on. Watch for sales and use coupons to further stretch your dollars. An important key is to buy what you normally eat. Doesn't do you any good to buy something simply because it was a great price if you won't eat it.

A big mistake that many people make is that they only buy "survival style foods" such as the military MRE's (Meals Ready to Eat) or massive cans of freeze dried soups or other choices. In my opinion both styles of items DO have

Stocking up one can or bottle at a time mounts up after a while.

a place in preparedness, but in their proper context -- not as a substitute for ordinary food such as say, canned beef stew and rice. For instance, you want to store some bulk wheat, a smart idea, so you run out and buy 300 pounds of it with the plan of next month buying 300 pounds of rice...well something catastrophic happens next week and all you have is 300 pounds of wheat. Can you live on it? Yes but for only a short time. If this is all you are giving your body, over time you will develop what is known as *appetite fatigue*. This means you simply cannot stand to eat that food any longer – you will take less and less of the food, and potentially end up in metabolic decline. You could literally starve to death sitting next to a bag of food.

In order to prevent this you must have as much balance in your diet as possible. Purchase and store what you usually eat just as was mentioned above. Staples are always a good idea, rice, pasta, beans, sugar, and flour among them. How many meals can you make with pasta? Well how many different kinds of topping/sauces do you have or can come up with from what you have on-hand right now? Spaghetti style sauce immediately comes to mind but what about, a cheese sauce, or a clam sauce or with some grilled veggies in a light olive oil? Something else to think about is how many different kinds of pasta are there? See what I mean? The variety (there's that word again) is amazing.

The human body is a remarkably resilient creation, but as amazing as it is throwing a monkey wrench in the works is not all that hard. Get the body undernourished, cold and wet and then try to function for extended periods. You can do it but it is tremendously harder. The goal is to increase both the quality and quantity of your options. (You may see this phrase again!) Your situation will likely mean you'll not be living in the lap of luxury, but so what? If you are warm, dry and had something filling to eat that could well put you far ahead of many of your neighbors.

The same statement about pasta is true of beans and rice. You can add salsa and cheese or, well, you get the point. You want meals to be flavorful and healthy.

Does it mean that you are going to be able to have

exactly what you want to eat any time you are hungry? Likely as not. depending on the situation. Do you have power? Are you at home? Are you on the road? What resources do you have available? How many are you trying to feed? These and other factors will influence the outcome. However, having supplies on-hand does mean that you can eat, and eat reasonably healthy.

The body needs fuel to function, and to maintain some balance in the body some of the fuel needs to be hot. There is also a psychological factor in this. If you can eat, especially if it is something warm, then your morale is maintained or even improved, your ability to think more clearly is increased and so on. It does have a positive trickle-down effect. There is a definite mental lift from even the smell of a hot meal cooking. Imagine the lift from actually eating it!

B) Remember to use **the FIFO rule** as it applies directly to food storage. It stands for *First In First Out*. That simply means the older items get used first to ensure longer shelf life and healthier eating. After you bring home groceries from the store and when putting them away place the newer items behind the older items of the same type. Think about it, you usually do this anyways without thinking about it. You bring home fresh fruit or vegetables you don't place them in front of the older ones! All this is doing is expanding that existing practice to all your food. You should also date the canned and dry goods with at least the month and year of purchase, using a marker. Makes it much easier to see what is older/newer at a glance. Less food is wasted, which translates to less wasted money.

C) **Decrease your debt**. This is easy to say, but for some it isn't as easy to do. Stop using your credit cards. Stop living above your means, if you are. Why do you NEED to have a brand new car when the three year old vehicle you have now works fine? Is it essential for your family to eat out six times a month or is it just you being lazy? Look at it like this, for the cost of three meals out for a family of four you can add a full months worth of food staples to your stocks. Are your utility bills up and down every month? Check with your utility company and see if they have a steady pay style plan. They average out your bills over a fixed period, usually a year and then that amount is what you pay every month. The advantage to this is you pay the same amount every month which allows you to better control your expenses. Do you have an adjustable rate mortgage? Refinance and get a fixed rate so that you will not get caught in a big jump in your payments.

Having a hard time with credit card debt? Look seriously into one of the many quality debt management firms that are operating today. They will sit down with you; take a look at your expenses, your debt and your income. If you qualify you will likely start saving as much as a few hundred dollars every month. You make one payment to them and they pay the credit card companies. A few catches with this, you will likely be required to give up your credit cards, zip, no more, they will be cut up and you will no longer have a bundle of plastic filling up your wallet or purse. Bear in mind some of the choices you might have to make to adjust to this lifestyle can seem harsh but in the long run, and this is about the long run, you will be better off without debt. How can having three hundred dollars less a month bleeding out your checkbook be a bad thing?

Most of these debt management firms also require that you do not take on any further debts such as new credit cards. Car loans, home loans etc are usually okay after a given period. Ask about this when you are first talking to them. These programs will take anywhere from three to six years to eliminate the debts but in the end that is a much shorter time than you trying to pay the cards off yourself. Another advantage is that some credit card companies will also lower your interest rate while in the program which saves you even more money since so much of your current monthly payment is just going to the interest.

D) Never allow your **vehicle gas tank** to fall below half. This way you are spending less to keep it topped off. Fuel supplies are notoriously vulnerable to shortages in times of crisis. Having a fuel tank that is over three quarters full gives you more options than one that is only at a quarter. Plus it costs less to keep it filled up which saves you money. With gas prices on the rise keeping as much fuel in your vehicle gives you more options. Don't forget the locking gas caps either!

E) **Store bottled water**, distilled water is best because it stores longer. Figure three gallons a day per person as an absolute minimum. This covers cooking, cleaning and hygiene needs for each person. Note I said "minimum" -- more is better. To further stretch your water supply it would also be good to store "non-potable" water, meaning this is not for human consumption. That water can be used for filling the toilet, pets etc. It is also highly recommended that you have the means to filter additional water.

F) Whenever possible **pay cash** for your purchases. This significantly reduces the paper trail from the store to your storeroom. An important point to be aware of is that stocking up ahead of time is NOT hoarding. Hoarding is when an individual takes more than their share following an event or crisis. Some people will have a different view on this especially after something happens and you have hot food and are staying warm and dry. They will feel, some of them quite strongly, that since you were better prepared than them that it your responsibility to take care of them. The entitlement mentality is strong in this country and it can lead to problems.

G) **Buy in bulk** – One of the best ways to save money when shopping is to buy in bulk. The growth of warehouse style stores such as Sam's Club © and Costco © around the country have made this much more convenient. They offer nationally known brands in larger size packages, multi-packs and case lots. I understand that buying in bulk isn't for everyone. What if there are only two people in the house? Or if you live in an apartment, rent a room or share a condo? I am not advocating this for everyone, it must be an individual choice. I am trying to make you aware of the choices that you have.

I am however strongly advocating in no uncertain terms that you should have absolutely as much food on-hand and the means to cook it safely as possible.

It is usually less expensive to buy one six pound

package of ground beef than it is to buy three two pound packages. Once at home you break the meat down into what size bundles you want and then vacuum seal them before sticking in the proper place in the freezer (remember FIFO). The vacuum sealer also saves you money by greatly reducing the risk of freezer burn to your meat and other food so that it stays good much longer and doesn't end up getting tossed out.

You can buy a flat of white button mushroom, clean them up and after running them through the dehydrator you can vacuum seal them up for long term storage. I have used mushrooms in sauces and other dishes that I dried and sealed as much as four years earlier with no problems. Compare that to the cost of buying canned mushrooms. The ways to use bulk buying to your advantage go far beyond what I have touched on here. Give it some thought and don't limit yourself.

-o-

Okay, you have sat down, looked at your situation, discussed the changes you are willing to commit to, and are ready to start making preparedness a lifestyle…so what happens now?

It makes sense to realize that in order to figure where you want to be that you find out where you're currently at in regards to how much food, water, etc you have on-hand. So to figure this out you need to take a written inventory. When you do this the first time it will take you longer because you are trying to gather up all the information and organize it. Don't let this scare you or slow you down. The key to is to be thorough, you really have to make sure that you write it all down.

Don't worry about categories, or breaking it down by item. We will do that later. Pick a spot in the kitchen or pantry and start counting. Green Beans, nine cans at 14.75 ounces; rice, two boxes at 28 ounces…and so on until you get the information written down. Be methodical, this is your life we are talking about. You can make a paper spreadsheet to record your information, or design one on your computer using a program like Excel, something like this chart here:

PRODUCT	NUMBER	SIZE OF PACKAGE
Green Beans	9 cans	14.75 oz
Rice, Instant	2 boxes	28 oz
etc	etc	etc

Once done with food, take a look at fuel, then move on to first aid supplies and so on. And then by the end of your list, you have a really decent idea of what you have. There is some terrific software out there that will help with this. One of the ones I am familiar with has a feature that will help you to figure out how much to stock based on the number of people, their gender and ages that are in the house. To make it easier on yourself don't try and do it all in one day. It is tedious, fair warning. Do some today, some tomorrow and so on.

-o-

An important note on this point and it immediately

relates back to food storage and more. It is absolutely vital that you do NOT advertise the fact before, during and to an extent after an event that you have supplies. Bragging to your friends, family and co-workers about how much food, water, fuel, weapons and ammunition, and so forth that you have stockpiled will lead to one of the following situations, I absolutely guarantee it.

"Well if something happens I know where I am going!" Then a dozen (think I am kidding?) people will be showing up at your house **demanding** (sometimes violently) that you share simply because you had the intelligence to stock up. There is NO incentive for them to stock up, since you already have. "But I am family, you HAVE to help me." Again, real world experience speaking-- not something to fill up this paragraph. Seen it, this DOES and WILL happen.

"Well if something happens I know where I am going and I will take what I need." If you think for a single second that there are those out there that don't feel this way then wake the hell up, right now. If you believe that Rob, who lives two houses over who hunts, would hesitate to shoot you because you are a nice guy -- to get at what you have when his kids are hungry -- you are sorely mistaken. Or one of your other neighbors or ... well, you get the idea. Folks, this is not fear mongering, or me being dramatic, to get you to do something. These are examples from real life of what has happened to people.

People are not rational, ethical or overly moral when they are dirty, hungry and scared. Fear is a powerful motivator, especially when that fear is being driven by a mob mentality. One of the comments I make often to many of my like minded friends is that following a major event it wouldn't be the criminal elements I would be most concerned about. I know they are out there, so be it. The ones I am most concerned about is a mob of hungry, once middle class, normally-decent people coming up the street looking for food. There are a great many more of them than criminals. They are my biggest concern.

A mob mentality strips those involved in it of their decency, their ethics and their inhibitions. Toss fear into the mix and the situation will get even uglier. Doubt me? Ask yourself this question and be honest with your answer: it is day six following a large scale event that struck your area and you still have no power, no food and little water, and the ability to get any of these things is basically zero. What lengths would you go to get your kids something to eat, drink or get them warm? You might not like the answer you come up with but if you are being honest it will give you some idea what people are capable of.

So broadcasting to the world that you are prepared is a bad idea. Low key, low profile. So what are some ways to do that and still buy what you need and keep it in the family? Space permitting in your home, put the bulk of your supplies and equipment in a non-traditional area such as the basement (if it is dry), in tubs under the beds, or the spare bedroom closet. One friend of mine and his wife stored some items in containers under their couch. Out of the way, out of sight, but easily accessible. This keeps it out of view from casual visitors. I get a laugh out of it every time I go over there, how many people have sat on that very couch not knowing they were sitting on supplies...

When shopping and you are buying a large amount, if someone – a clerk, another shopper -- asks why, simply tell them:

- *It is none of their business. Don't be rude but be firm.*

- *Tell the person asking that you're shopping for your local church group and upgrading their food stocks or getting ready for a large group meal.*

- *Your family is having a large gathering and you have been elected to cook.*

- *Your family is planning a camping trip involving several people and you want to make sure you have enough.*

- *Want to get the family cabin stocked up.*

These are a few examples of what you can say; the list goes on and on. The truth is most people won't prep but they will remember that you do. You need to practice what the military refers to as operational security or OPSEC for short. What that means in basic terms is having a system that protects your information. Don't brag about how long you can survive in an event, don't talk up your new purchases, and don't do anything that brings the light of attention onto you and your family. Have a discussion with your children, what goes on in the house stays at home. My wife and I used this rule with our kids. It is not anyone else's business what we bought or stored.

The neighborhood kids were not allowed in my

garage at all since this is where we stored large amounts of our supplies. We used the line, "it is not a play area" to aid with this. When service people come to your home, restrict their movements, keep doors to rooms they are not in closed. What you have is YOUR business, no one else's.

So trying to prepare is a series of steps and all of them are important so settle in for the long haul -- and don't forget that the process can and should be fun as well.

-o-

NOTES

2 FOOD

Okay, here is what at first glance may seem an easy subject: food. Something we are all familiar with and enjoy. So how does this seemingly easy topic fit into preparedness? Simple, without it we die, no muss, no fuss, no food, no life. Have your attention now? I hope so.

Here are a few points that I would like to take a moment or two to address. During the time of the Great Depression a much higher percentage of people in this country grew their own gardens, raised livestock and poultry, and made their own clothes to meet the needs of their own families. Family groups were also usually much closer together geographically speaking, which allowed for greater support of all types. Today neither of these factors are the same. Depending upon whose figures you use only one to two percent of the US population feeds the rest of us! Think about that for a second: you have one or two people feeding themselves and the other ninety eight...scary ratio.

Understand that a farmer in, say, Kansas produces a crop of wheat. This wheat is harvested by the farmer then taken to a mill and processed into flour. The flour is then sometimes taken to a holding location known as an elevator or right to a bakery. At the bakery it is made into a loaf of bread, a bag of rolls, or whatever. From the bakery it is taken straight to a store or it might even go to a regional distribution center first before going on to a store -- and from there to someone's home.

So if at any point in this process, any point, if there is a break in the chain or even a delay, then the bread is not sitting on the shelf at the store. This process is similar, but of course not exactly, to how every product gets to our markets -- but you get the idea. What I am talking about here is how susceptible the agricultural infrastructure is. So many stores use the JIT (Just In Time) inventory system. This means that what you see on grocery shelves is all that they have -- unlike in days past when a store would have a large volume of goods and food in the back warehouse.

A large run on a grocery store by panicked shoppers can easily wipe out a store in less than a few hours. This is a well proven fact here in the United States. Think about the news reports that come from hurricane areas every year as folks invariably wait till the last minute then decide "Oh, better go get a few things." Not a smart way to do it at all. It is much better to do the buying well in advance of a potential crisis. How do we do that, you ask?

Specifically set aside however many dollars a week

you are comfortable with for purchasing additional groceries, concentrating on items that you already eat now. One big thing to mention at this point is buy ingredients, not pre-prepared foods. Ingredients will last longer and it allows you greater variety in how you use the food. Buy tuna, rice, sugar, pasta (so many great choices there!), canned soups (also an area of tremendous choices), and canned vegetables. The addition of these weekly purchases will steadily but consistently add to your on-hand amount. Don't forget things like baking soda, yeast, baking powder and shortening as well since these items will be needed to further stretch the food. Get a good food storage cookbook to help you as well.

-o-

Following is a basic listing of food. Much of it you may have in your home already. What proper preparedness is about is having what you use on a regular basis, on-hand, in greater quantities. So in taking a look at the listing we see that it covers a variety of dietary situations. You will see staples, condiments, spices, ingredients for snacks, desserts and baking. The reason for this is to allow for the most flexibility in your meal preparations both now and following an event if necessary.

Obviously one of the vital elements of preparing food is having the means to heat the ingredients to the proper temperature. This can be done using your electric stove (if there is power) or your gas range (if there is gas) or it could using your propane or charcoal BBQ grill, or maybe you have a camping style stove. Then, there is using the wood stove that you normally heat the house with…See how many options you have? More than you thought?

Baking mixes (*Pie crust plus canned pie filling equals cobbler*)
Baking powder
Baking soda
Barley
Bay leaves (*delicious in beans, and insects avoid foods like flour with a bay leaf stored inside the bag*)
Beans-dry
Bottled drinks and juices (*not refrigerated type*)
Brown Sugar
Bullion, concentrated broth
Butter flavoring, (*Molly McButter, freeze for storage if you can.*)
Candy
Canned beans
Canned broth (beef, chicken)
Canned chicken breast
Canned chili
Canned diced tomatoes, other tomato products, and sauces
Canned French fried onions
Canned fruit
Canned milk, evaporated milk
Canned pie filling
Canned pumpkin
Canned Salmon
Canned soups
Canned stew
Canned sweet potatoes

Canned Tuna
Canned veggies
Cans of lemonade mix, other canned dry drink mixes
Cheese dips in jars
Cheese soups, like cheddar, broccoli cheese, and jack cheese
Chinese food ingredients
Chocolate bars
Chocolate chips
Chocolate syrup, strawberry syrup squeeze bottles
Coffee filters (*also for straining silt out of water*)
Corn Masa de Harina or corn tortilla mix
Corn meal
Corn starch for thickening
Crackers
Cream of Wheat
Cream soups (*good for flavoring rice & pasta*)
Crisco
Dried eggs
Dried fruit
Dried onion (*big containers at warehouse stores*)
Dried soups
Dry cocoa
Dry coffee creamer (*big sealed cans, many uses including making dry milk taste better*)
Dry milk powder
Dry Mustard
Flour, self rising flour tortilla mix for flour tortillas, wraps, and flatbread
Garlic powder
Granola bars (not great shelf life)

Hard candy
Honey
Hot chocolate mix
Instant coffee if you drink it, or coffee and a manual drip cone or similar
Instant mashed potatoes
Jarred or canned spaghetti sauce
Jarred peppers
Jellies and Jams
Jerky
Ketchup
Kool Aid
Lard, Manteca (*good in beans, substitute for bacon or salt pork, tortilla making, many other uses*)
Large packages dry pasta, thinner type saves fuel
Marshmallow cream
Marshmallows
Mayo packets from warehouse store, if you must, not really a good value.
Mexican food ingredients
Mustard
Nestle Table Cream (*substitute for sour cream, cream, or half-and-half in lots of ethnic stores, including British*)
Nuts (*freeze if you have room*)
Oatmeal
Oil (*Shelf life not great*)
Olive oil
Olives, green and black
Onion powder
Packaged bread crumbs

Parmesan cheese
Peanut butter, nut butters
Pepper
Pet food
Pickles, relish (not refrigerator case type)
Powdered sugar
Power bars
Raisins
Ramen style noodles
Ravioli or any canned pasta
Real butter or favorite margarine-(*keep frozen until disaster if you can. Butter keeps a long time in cool temps*)
Rice
Salsa and hot sauces
Salt
Spam or Treet
Spices and herbs your family likes
Stovetop Dressing mix
Sugar
Summer sausage (*cheaper around holidays*)
Sweetened condensed milk
Syrups
Tea bags
Trail mix
Tuna (*in water not oil*)
Ultra pasteurized milk (*expensive*)
Vanilla (*improves dry milk, too*)
Velveeta (*watch carton date, freeze for storage if possible*)
Vienna sausage
Yeast, (*keep it cool or put in freezer*)

Okay, you have looked over the list and said, wow, that is a heck of a lot of stuff. Yes it is. But, if you have already done your inventory (as we talked about in the previous chapter) you realized that you, like most households in the United States, already have the majority of these items on-hand even if the quantities aren't very high yet. Plus not everything on the list has to be on-hand depending on taste preferences or even cultural or religious guidelines.

I made the list as long as possible to cover as many dietary choices as possible. What we need to do now is to identify what you want/need, don't have, get it, and add to what you do have to increase your options.

Food storage area for one family.

See the photo which shows a section of the food storage from one family. Much of it is recognizable brands and products. This picture shows one corner of the storage room. Like items are group together and the arrangement on the shelves allows easy access for proper rotation of goods.

Get up right now and go to the kitchen or pantry. Once there, grab a can of vegetables, any kind, doesn't matter. What you are looking for is what is known as the "use by date." This date is often on the bottom of the can and will say some version of "Best by Jan 31 13." What is important to understand is that this date is a *guideline*. It is not an absolute; it is the manufacturers recommended date to use the product by.

Federal regulations require food manufacturers to place a "Use By" date on their products. Canned goods are one of the true marvels of an industrial society, it allows for the safe storage and handling of perishable food. Canned goods when **properly** stored will last for years. The keys to proper long-term storage of canned goods include:

- *Keeping the cans in a cool, dry environment with as consistent temperature control as possible.*

- *Do NOT use cans that are dented as the seal of the container may be compromised.*

- *Never use canned goods that have swelled. This is a sign of botulism which is a deadly serious health problem. If you find a can in this condition discard it immediately.*

This shows another storage room. Visible are many side dishes as well as some of the staples such as rice and pasta (in the plastic drawers to the left).

What Are Some Other Helpful Food Storage Tips?

Store your rice in empty CLEAN two liter pop bottle, they store well, last longer than in their regular container and are easy to handle and transport.

Store spices, condiments and gravy mixes as well as food. This will make it much easier for the staple to go further since the meals will have great taste and variety using the same basic ingredients.

Store multi-vitamins, as well as food, to supplement your diet and energy levels.

Food Safety Tips

Once upon a time I was the Safety/Security Director for a federally owned facility. As part of my responsibilities I was required to conduct inspections of both of the commercial kitchens that operated on the premises. In order to properly do this, I attended one of the ServSafe Food Sanitation courses conducted by the National Restaurant Association. This was an intense two day course followed by a proctored exam. There were a number of topics covered during the course that I felt would be good to pass along.

Food safety cannot be overlooked; this is especially true in a preparedness scenario. Manpower might be limited already and if someone or a group suffers from a food borne illness then the entire situation can become untenable.

To better acquaint you with food safety let's start with a basic questionnaire to test your knowledge. **Answers are at the end of the chapter.**

- *Do you know what the temperature danger zone is for food?*
- *What is the ideal temperature range for frozen food to be held at?*
- *What are the conditions that favor the growth of food borne microorganisms?*
- *What is the minimum internal temperature that needs to be reached for Beef? Chicken? Fish?*
- *Can you identify at least three foods or food types that the FDA (Food and Drug Administration) identifies as potentially hazardous foods? (Hint: there are at least 11 of these)*

One of the facts stressed during the course was that sanitation is not only a good idea, it is essential to help to *reduce* the likelihood of contamination. Please note the previous sentence does NOT say *eliminate* the likelihood. If food is exposed to the air, which is pretty much a given, then the potential for contamination is always present. Food borne illness is caused by several factors which can be placed into one of three categories: time-temperature abuse, cross-contamination, and poor personal hygiene. Now let's take a closer look at these three factors:

Time-Temperature Abuse

This is when food is allowed to remain for too long at temperatures favorable to the growth of microorganisms. Common factors in this are:
- Failure to hold or store food at required temperatures.
- Failure to cook or reheat foods to temperatures that kill microorganisms.
- Failure to properly cool foods.
- Preparation of foods a day or more before they are served.

Cross-contamination

This is when microorganisms are transferred from one surface or food to another. Examples of this include:

- Adding raw, contaminated ingredients to foods that receive no further cooking.
- Food contact surfaces (equipment or utensils) that are not cleaned and sanitized before touching cooked or ready to eat foods.

- Allowing raw food to touch or drip fluids onto cooked or ready to eat foods.
- Hands that touch contaminated (usually raw) foods and then touch cooked or ready to eat foods.
- Contaminated cleaning cloths that are not cleaned and sanitized before being used on other food-contact surfaces.

Poor Personal Hygiene
Examples of this include but are not limited to:
- Failure to properly wash hands after using the restroom or whenever necessary.
- Coughing or sneezing on or near food.
- Touching or scratching sores, cuts, or boils then touching food without washing hands.

Ensuring Food Safety

The key to food safety lies in controlling time and temperature throughout the food handling process, practicing good personal hygiene, and preventing cross contamination. How do we do these things? Since microorganisms pose the largest threat to food safety limiting or eliminating the chance of growth is a major step. Controlling time and temperature is essential to limit growth.

The following is designed to show how to move food through the process. These steps are just as important in the home as they are in restaurants and other locations where food is handled and/or prepared so please don't assume this isn't for you.

Step One - RECEIVING

Receive and store food quickly

Step Two - STORAGE

Store foods at their recommended temperatures

Step Three - PREPARATION

Minimize the time food spends in the temperature danger zone of 41 F to 140 F

Step Four - COOKING

Cook food to its minimum internal temperature for the appropriate amount of time

Step Five - HOLDING

Hold hot foods at 140 F or higher and cold foods at 41 F or lower

Step Six - COOLING

Cool cooked foods to 70 F within two hours and 70 F to 41 F or below in an additional four hours

Step Seven - REHEATING

Reheat foods to an internal temperature of 165 F for fifteen seconds within two hours

Food Handling Points

- *Keep contact surfaces (equipment, utensils, cutting boards, etc) clean and sanitary*

- *Always wash your hands and avoid wearing excessively soiled clothing while cooking or preparing food*

- *Do not allow raw food to drip on or touch cooked or ready to eat food*

-o-

The greatest threat to food safety is microorganisms. Microorganisms are responsible for the majority of food borne-illness outbreaks. There are four types of micro-organisms that can contaminate food and cause food borne illness: bacteria, viruses, parasites and fungi. These microorganisms can be arranged into two groups: spoilage microorganisms and pathogens (disease causing). For example mold is a type of spoilage microorganism. On the other side of the coin is Salmonella which is a pathogen.

In order for microorganisms (except viruses) to grow, certain conditions are needed. These conditions can be easily remembered with the acronym FAT-TOM which stands for: *Food, Acid, Time - Temperature, Oxygen* and *Moisture*.

Food - Microorganisms need nutrients, specifically proteins and carbohydrates.

Acid - The microorganisms do not grow well in foods that are highly acidic or highly alkaline.

Temperature - Most food borne microorganisms grow well between the temperatures of 41 F and 140 F. This range is known as the danger zone.

Time - Microorganisms need time to grow. In the right environment, bacteria can double their population every 20 minutes.

Oxygen - Most microorganisms that cause food borne illness can grow with (aerobic) or without (anaerobic) the presence of oxygen.

Moisture - Most food borne microorganisms grow well in moist food.

-o-

How do we protect ourselves from microorganisms? One way is having multiple barriers.

- *Make Food more acidic* - Add vinegar, lemon juice, lactic acid or another kind of citrus

- *Raise or Lower the temperature of the Food* - Move food out of the danger zone by keeping it above 140 F or below 40 F.

- *Lower the water activity of the Food* - Dry food by adding sugar, salt, alcohol or acid. Food can also be freeze or air dried to remove water.

- *Lessen the amount of time the Food is in the temperature danger zone* - Prepare food as close to the time of service as possible.

Something else to consider is having oversized cookware on-hand. If you are cooking for a larger than usual amount of people it makes the process much easier.

A few words of caution

If a serious situation does arise that creates food shortages a major concern would be groups of people raiding homes searching for food. I would strongly recommend not having all your food stored in the same location in the house. You could store some in unlikely places such as under the beds (use plastic containers to make getting the food in and out easier), hide some in the garage (be wary of temperature conditions, hot weather greatly shortens the shelf life), use the basement or crawlspace if you have an interior access.

When it comes to dealing with roving groups demanding food you have a couple of choices.

Take it with you – if you leave take as much with you as possible, but understand that leaving could mean your unprotected home will get looted at some point.

Hide it – have some left out that the group can find and hope that they will be satisfied with that.

Defend it – a difficult choice but it may be your last option, especially if no resupply is likely.

SUMMARY

Tens of thousands of people in the United States suffer from some type of food borne illness every year. If the outbreak is serious enough we hear about it on the national news, some people die, which CAN be prevented. Common sense and some awareness goes a long way to reducing your chances of becoming ill. In a SHTF situation there will be enough to worry about -- how effective are you going to be if you and/or your team are seriously ill due to contaminated food?

- *Keep food out of the danger zone 40 F - 140 F.*
- *Keep contact areas and utensils clean and sanitary.*
- *Wash your hands before and after handling food.*
- *Do not allow raw food to mix with prepared food.*
- *It is YOUR health and the health of those you care about.*

Answers to Questions

Danger zone is 40 F to 140 F

Ideal Freezer Temp is from -10 F up to 10 F

Conditions - FAT-TOM

Internal Temperatures Beef 155 F, Chicken 165 F, Fish 160 F

Potentially Hazardous Foods - Tofu, Meat (lamb, beef, pork), milk and dairy products, cooked rice, beans or other heat treated plant foods, soy-protein foods, fish, poultry, sliced melons, baked or boiled potatoes, shellfish and other crustacean, shelled eggs, sprouts and raw seeds, and garlic and oil mixtures.

-o-

3 WATER

One of the most important means of helping to maintain our own health and well being involves keeping our bodies well hydrated. A large portion of our tissue is liquid of different types. These liquids must be replenished by the body on a regular basis to help keep itself in balance and operating efficiently.

Clean water is first and foremost on that short list of necessary liquids. Please note I said "clean" water. Drinking water that is contaminated can quickly lead to a variety of problems. The body is an amazing machine of incredible precision, it can at times operate under less than ideal circumstances but it cannot do it well for extended periods. Think about it like tossing a wrench into a machine, not a good idea. A good way to think about the need for water is by using the Rule of Threes:

You can live three minutes without oxygen
You can live three days without water
You can live three weeks without food

Having an adequate supply of water on-hand can prove difficult for some because water is both bulky in size as well as heavy. For the vast majority of people in the United States their water is provided by some manner of municipal delivery system. These systems are heavily dependent upon electricity, if there is no power then there is no water. It is true that many cities and towns have back-up power supplies on-hand to serve in case of power outages but these back-ups require human inter-action to be maintained. If the event which caused the power outage is severe enough such as a large tornado or earthquake then the people needed for the system to stay operational may not be able to reach the locations or be able to repair the damage in a timely manner.

It is possible that there will be water pressure for some time after an event but it is important to understand that it may disappear without notice. There will be some residual water pressure in the system but as people flush their toilets, run their sinks it will quickly bleed off and be gone. If you live or work in a high rise building forget it, water will not flow upward without pumps to create the needed hydraulic pressure which brings the water up. In addition, contaminated water may backflow into systems, making the water unusable.

Waterborne Illnesses

One of the jobs that municipal water departments are responsible for is the treatment of our drinking water to remove harmful chemicals, heavy metals, toxins and bacteria. Without these treatments many people around the country would become ill and some of those would die as a result. Those most at risk are young children and elderly due to their immune systems not being able to properly handle the problem.

How to Purify Water?

Okay, you understand that having water is essential. Fine, you have access to water that you are not sure is safe to drink so how to make it safe to drink? There are several proven methods of purifying water.

- *Boiling* – Bring the water to a rolling boil for at least 30 seconds
- *Chemical treatment* – Iodine or 8 -16 drops of unscented bleach per gallon
- *Filtration* – The finer the filter screen the better

How Much Water?

An important question to consider is how much water do you need to plan on having for each person in your family/group? A rule that I use for planning is an absolute minimum of three gallons person per day. Please note that I said minimum. There are a number of factors that could easily make this a much higher number. If for example you live in the desert southwest, you should plan on at least an additional gallon per person per day due to heat extremes.

There is no absolute answer to this question because where you live, your age, your health, the availability of water and more all play a role in how much water to store. Don't forget to factor in water for your pets and any other animals also. For example, a cow will require a gallon of water for each half gallon of milk she produces – about a bathtub full of water *each day.*

Water storage isn't your own option, the ability to filter water is important. There are a number of quality water filtration products out there ranging in cost from reasonable to expensive – British Berkefeld filters, AquaRain, Katadyn, all are good.

A "Big Berkey" in daily use.

If you are handy, you can make your own perfectly functional filter system with clean builder's sand piled deeply over drain tiles within a large basin (such as a 50 gallon plastic trash can or a rain barrel). At the drain tile level at the bottom of the basin, install a drain so you can draw off water. This is called a "slow sand filter" and is one of the simple technologies recommended by the World

Health Organization in third world countries to help clean drinking water.

Slow sand filters are gravity fed and don't require chemicals or electricity. They can be cleaned by drying the sand in bright sunlight and turning it repeatedly OR it's possible to clean the filter by "wet harrowing" (scraping the sand while still in the water, then draining that water so it isn't used for drinking). The water does need to be fairly clear to start with – so filter it through cheesecloth, sheets, or by letting it settle for several days before pouring into the filter. Personally, I'd still add a bit of chlorine bleach to this to make sure all biological contaminants were neutralized.

A note on this (and not just for water filtration products) expensive doesn't always mean quality and affordable doesn't always mean low quality. Do your research. A great website for more information is **www.homespunenvironmental.com**.

One of the best sources for water comes from above us in the form of rain. A good rainwater collection system tied into regular household guttering can yield surprisingly high amounts of water. Use this simple formula – *multiply the square footage of roof collection space you have available X 0.6 gallons per square foot per inch of rain* to come up with the total you could collect.

A note on this, some states consider it illegal for homeowners to install rainwater collections systems because the rainwater is considered state property. Check the laws in your area.

Now if you do collect the rainwater I highly recommend that you purify it before you use it for drinking or cooking. It can be filtered by any of the systems recommended, or you may add plain household bleach (make sure there are no fragrances added) at the rate of 8 drops of bleach per gallon of clear water, and 16 drops per gallon of murky water. Let it sit for at least an hour before use.

Use opaque containers to reduce algae growth as well. Rainwater is fine for use in the toilet or on the garden as well. I know several people who have large capacity collection systems set up around their properties.

Water is essential to what we need to do. Another way of phrasing the importance of this one item is: *without water, it doesn't matter what else you have.*

-o-

4 POWER

One of the greatest needs during a crisis may be electrical power. Electrical energy to drive a well pump or a respiratory machine for a loved one, the ability to cook some food, energize a radio to help transmit a request for assistance or listen for news of a missing family member...the list is virtually endless. We have created a society that is based on electricity. The need for power generation cannot be overstated.

For instance in 1995 a severe heat wave lasting several days hit Chicago. Despite having electricity available it's estimated that at least 600 people died in a five day period. Some estimates place the number higher. Most of those who perished were elderly who didn't have air conditioning at all or didn't use it out of fear of the cost of the power. These people died when there were operating power grids. If there had not been power the number of dead would have been much, much higher. Again, please bear in mind that these deaths occurred with social organization operating and power available.

To better understand what we are talking about it is necessary to do a short review on the ins and outs of electrical power. Standard household electrical current is 110 volts AC which stands for (A)lternating (C)urrent. Direct Current (DC) is what our vehicles produce and so an adaptor, better known as an *inverter,* is called for. There are appliances that are wired to operate on DC power. A popular source for these are truck stops since many over-the-road truckers have these in their rigs to allow them have coffee, cook dinner, and much more. You might be surprised at the variety of DC appliances that are available.

The means to generate electrical power comes in a variety of forms. I would recommend a combination of these methods to help ensure that whatever the situation is you have some power available to you. The options for power include:

- *Grid Power* – This is the normal electrical power that is supplied from municipal sources.
- *Solar* – Created by photo-galvanic panels and converted into alternating current (AC) power from direct current (DC).
- *Wind* – A windmill generates DC power which is converted to AC power for usage.
- *Hydrodynamic* – Water flow is used to generate DC power which is converted to AC.
- *Generator* – Creates AC power and the units can be fixed in place or portable.

Following is a generalized overview of each of the options. There are more Pro and Con for each but this is designed as a quick reference for you listing what I feel are the most common pluses and minuses for each.

Grid Power

PRO	CON
Familiar, easy to use	If grid goes down, no main power
Someone else helps pay the upkeep cost and does maintenance	Limited control of cost to you
Available in nearly all areas	Weather affected due to size of grid

Solar Power

PRO	CON
Many styles of panels including shingles	Doesn't charge at night, poorly on cloudy days
Rebates and/or tax credits often available for part of cost	Can be expensive to install system
Limited amount of upkeep needed	System is hard to hide, no OPSEC

Wind Power

PRO	CON
Can produce power anytime there's wind	System is hard to hide, no OPSEC
Refunds often available for part of cost	Doesn't produce as much power as solar

Hydrodynamic Power

PRO	CON
System is quiet	MUST have nearby river/stream with constant flow
Refunds often available for part of cost	Doesn't produce as much as power as solar
Can produce power around the clock	Can be expensive to install

Generator Power

PRO	CON
Many are portable, you can take with you	Noisy which alerts others to you
Multi-fuel options for some models	Requires some type of fuel
Only runs when you want it to	Might not produce enough power

One note on generators: most of them come equipped with a spark arrestor assembly on the end of the exhaust pipe. This is in comparison to a muffler whose purpose is to reduce noise. Having a generator is a smart idea but running it when there is little to no ambient "city" noise to dampen the sound could prove dangerous. I highly recommend you remove the spark arrestor assembly and replace it with a muffler. Small engine mufflers are inexpensive and often very easy to change out. Check your local auto parts stores for mower mufflers. The noise reduction is often significant and further improves your overall operational security. I was very embarrassed when a friend of mine pointed out this oversight on my own generator -- which I corrected. A word to the wise.

So, there are a number of power choices available. As I stated above a combination of these options is really your best way to go. I want to stress that your initial cost could be high depending on how in-depth your purchases are. To help offset that cost many states and even some utility companies offer partial rebates on the cost of the system. Check your jurisdiction for more information on this. Another benefit of alternate power is that some states require the utility companies to buy electricity that is surplus to your needs. So if your system produces more power than what you use and store, you can sell the power back to the grid -- which further helps to reimburse your costs.

Determining your power needs, to decide how much to generate, isn't as hard as it may seem. Many appliances list how much power they use. An inexpensive device that is available and easy to use is known as the Kill A Watt (P3

International) which allows you to measure how much power an individual appliance utilizes. This unit is very cost effective and easy to use.

You can also get a rough figure of your power needs by checking each appliance near where the electrical cord enters the device – it will state something like:

1440W   120VAC   60HZ

That means that the device (in this case, a counter-top toaster oven) uses 1,440 WATTS of 120 VOLT ALTERNATING CURRENT which runs at 60 HERTZ (cycles per second). All household appliances use 120 VAC at 60 HZ, since that is the grid standard. The 1,440 W is how much "juice" the oven draws when it is running – in other words, it is a juice hog!

In a grid down situation, using this oven would require almost as much energy as a conventional electric oven, or a portable electric heater – and way more than a microwave. The microwave might pull 1,440 W, but it only runs for seconds to minutes at a time, making it a more energy-efficient device if you need something like this.

Add together the wattage of all the electric things you use (TV, radio, stereo, microwave, dishwasher, heater, air conditioner, fans, electric lights, freezer, refrigerator, wine coolers, etc.) for the total use if everything was on at the same time.

-o-

Once you have determined how much power you need, I would like to take a moment to clarify something.

Determining how much power you need vs. how much power you want is important. There are appliances and such that you will need to have operational at least at times, such as the well pump, freezer, refrigerator and some lights. This is in contrast to having all of the previously mentioned units and a stereo, the computer, a hair dryer and other non-essential appliances running at once. A question you need to ask yourself is what *must* I have the ability to keep powered vs. what do I *want* to keep powered. Nothing wrong with having some music going, a solar powered battery charger will do nicely to keep a small CD player going.

A freezer for example does not need to powered 24/7. You can keep its internal temperature relatively stable by running it for 2-3 hours at a time at least three times a day and minimizing the number of times you are in and out of it. However if you have a solar system with a well maintained battery bank you can reduce the headaches without firing up the generator. Since it is silent there is no concern about someone hearing it, which helps with your security. Speaking of that, another item that could be well worth the time and power to keep going is a few (or all) of your exterior security cameras and the monitor. These could be a huge help in keeping an eye on things.

So now that you have determined how much power you need you can shop for a generator and some solar panels if you're so inclined. When doing your calculations on how much electrical capacity to have on-hand give yourself a buffer of at least 15% over what your total needs are. No reason to not have a cushion in this area. Better to have the extra and not need it.

NOTES

5 FIRST AID

** This is an important note to begin this section, and one that can help to keep you out of legal trouble. You should **never** administer medical care beyond the scope of your training. To do so could very likely place you in a situation making you civilly liable and potentially criminally negligent. Most states have a Good Samaritan law on the books which states (this is* **not** *the legal definition) that a person acting in good faith cannot be held liable for any harm they cause while rendering aid. Research your state law and local laws regarding this. An additional facet of this is that in some states as a trained responder you are legally obligated to render aid. Consult your local laws. **

The need for medical training and supplies cannot be overstated. For me, first aid supplies are one of those cannot-have-too-many-of kinds of things. It has been seen time and time again following disasters of all types' people waiting in line for medical treatment because they lacked even the basic supplies such as bandages or just some gauze to treat their own wounds. This lack of preparedness ties up medical personnel who could be spending their time treating those who are really injured. Imagine, not being able to treat some basic injuries such as cuts on your own? That is ridiculous and inexcusable.

I was certified at the EMT–Intermediate level for several years and so my own stock of medical supplies and equipment is larger than what might be found in the average home. I have a large First Aid kit in my vehicle plus a household kit, and a good stock of spare supplies which allows me to restock whatever is used. Much of the regular supplies such as Band-Aids, medications, and hydrogen peroxide were purchased at the local Wal-Mart. That kept costs down. My son, like many other children, is active so he comes home with his share of cuts, scrapes, bumps and bruises that require some attention and keeps my skill levels up.

As a rule I have always tried to keep a decent amount of supplies on-hand but a few years into my marriage my wife and I decided to increase our stock. We wanted the means to more easily restock what might be used, and a larger variety of supplies in case of something disrupting the ability to replace supplies. So after gathering up all the materials and equipment on-hand we completed an inventory. Then we placed a good-sized order with a firm in the mid-west that I had done business with in the past. Since it was right around tax return time it used up about $250 worth of the refund to buy supplies. Obviously, this is no small amount. But given what my wife and I wanted to add to our personal stock, this was an amount we were comfortable with.

Much of what we purchased and had delivered could have gotten at Wal-Mart or a similar retail outlet but by buying in bulk we were able to save quite a bit and stretch our funds much further. The $250 or so we spent really did go a long way, the order was delivered in three good size boxes. It took me nearly one full evening to sort it all out, organize what I wanted to go in what kit and put all three kits together. What was left over became our resupply stock. It really came in handy when we divorced because we were able to split our overall stock and it provided each of us with a large amount.

What I did for the two vehicle kits was to buy two large (23 x 10.5 x 8.5 inches) tool boxes made of a rigid plastic at a local hardware store for about eight dollars each. Since there was several color choices available I selected red to better distinguish it from the other tool box in each of the vehicles which oddly enough actually contains tools. The tool kit is rugged, easy to carry with one hand and holds enough supplies to be able to treat a wide variety of injuries on several people at once if necessary. The handy lift out tray is perfect for smaller items like tape, shears, and containers of hand sanitizer and so on. Below the tray is where the bulk of the supplies rest.

One thing I did then, and continue to do, is make sure that each kit has a large number of gloves in them in both large and extra large sizes. These are kept in the center of the kit immediately below the tray as a reminder that if there is the need to treat someone with any type of body fluid present, that we need to protect ourselves. To keep the various supplies accessible and to maintain quality, I used zip lock style sandwich bags. They are see through, tear resistant, inexpensive (there's that word again) and re-sealable which makes them almost ideal.

An excellent list of recommended medical supplies is provided at the end of this book. The list is a starting point for you to begin with as you assemble your own stock of medical supplies. My deep thanks to Carrie Williams, Paramedic, for use of the listing which she compiled.

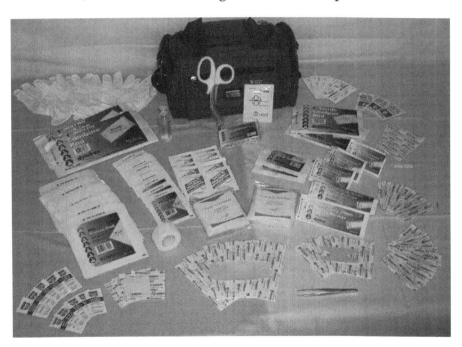

An example of a commercially available first aid
(courtesy of Southern Plains Consulting)

Something to bear in mind is that the list is the recommended absolute minimum amounts especially with items such as dressings. I know from experience that wound care can eat through a large amount of disposable items such as dressings and gauze. For instance, a large gash on the leg properly dressed and cared for might use up as many as thirty gauze dressings while it heals. So having more on-hand is important.

Something else my wife and I had done over the years was to accumulate a variety of medical equipment such as a used but very serviceable wheelchair, a walker, a pair of crutches, a military style litter for transporting wounded and an assortment of joint splints / supports. Our intention with this was that if something does happen we'd have as much on-hand to help ourselves as possible. If it is not needed for us then we can provide it for someone else. The benefits of helping others should not be overlooked so long as you remember to ensure your own security, especially following an incident.

Much of what we acquired was from unlikely sources. The wheelchair was being thrown out by a hospital because one of the screws holding the seat on had broken off. I drilled out the offending item and had a new screw in place in less than ten minutes. The litter I bought at a military surplus store for $45 which I felt was a bargain. The crutches were from an injury one of the kids had and we were given by the hospital. The rest we picked up as the opportunity presented itself.

In the case of a serious event that keeps the normal community infrastructure from operating the ability to offer medical skills could literally be a life saver. The injured person could be someone in your family, your neighbor, or even you. I served for a time as a Red Cross volunteer working with the county disaster response team. One of the things we constantly strived toward was ensuring that following any event that we would be able to travel to the site, set up, and be functioning as rapidly as possible. If in the midst of chaos an oasis of order appears, then people will gravitate toward it. So if you have the ability to perform medical functions (again, staying within your training) it places you in the position of being someone that can help others. A good part of the reason I took the EMT training was that I was tired of not knowing what to do when a situation arose.

Many situations involving some measure of medical knowledge are those for simple injuries such as cuts, scrapes, or mild burns. Other situations you may run across will likely involve some degree of training. The good news is that the training may be much more available than you know. Speak with the local chapter of Red Cross, the fire department/rescue squad or your community college.

Medical training is not difficult but does require some commitment. I cannot encourage you enough to not only check on this but follow through and attend some training. The more the better, depending upon your employer you might be able to get tuition assistance or reimbursement for the training. I was able to do that for my initial EMT training which made it that much better. When I took my classes to become a CPR Instructor my volunteer fire department paid for half the cost of the class, which made it easier for me to get the training.

So take a look at what you have, think about what you want to have and go out and get some training. I promise you it will be worth the time and effort. The life you may save could be your own.

Medical Training

In order to adequately handle medical situations now or following some type of event you may need to undergo training to gain the skills you will need. One note on this is that to render First Aid is like many acquired skills: it needs to be practiced. Does this mean stand around with a First Aid kit slung over your shoulder waiting for some poor devil to sustain an injury? Of course not but in this regard I am speaking of volunteering at sporting events or with the local Fire or Emergency Squad, being a chaperone at school events, reading up on appropriate literature and in general keeping yourself as current on the medical information as possible.

There are several levels of training that exist in the medical community. I am talking here about those below the level of doctors and nurses.

First Responders – (Lowest Level)

Emergency Medical Technicians -(Basic)

Emergency Medical Technicians - (Intermediate)

Paramedics

Each of the levels talked about above require more and more training just as it describes. Not everyone has the desire to be a Paramedic, the money nor the time to undertake the training. Another factor is where is the training being offered? In many areas of the country would be students who do not have easy access to the training they desire. A very smart friend of mine summed it up to me like this, "The more you know, the less you need," and this adage would certainly apply in this area.

-o-

6 SHELTER

What I want to do now is talk about something that is more complex than it might seem at first glance, shelter. Humans are driven to find shelter; it is something innate to our being. We must have shelter of some type in order to function better. Depending on where you are, what you are doing, and the things you have, along with the seasons, will influence the shelter you will have access to or should you have to, construct.

How does this relate to preparedness? Well, we have talked about how having additional options increases your survival chances, So as it were shelter is just another option and is absolutely a major part of the overall. I feel it would be safe to state, in my opinion, that the majority of the people in this country consider their home (whether they realize it or not) as their primary shelter. This is also true for myself.

We don't tend to think about it in that regard but, that may be due to the fact that we take it for granted. Our homes, whether it's a traditional house, a condominium, apartment, maybe even a recreational vehicle or manufactured home, is where we will have most of our belongings and it is where we are often the most comfortable. By that I'm not talking about physical comfort, which is important I concede, but what I am referring to here is a state of mental familiarity. It's where we eat, spend time with our family, sleep and because that is where the majority of our belongings are it provides us with the mental state that lets us know we belong there.

So in a preparedness sense, being aware of that gives us a starting place. Take a moment and give some thought to your primary residence. Is it a house, apartment, condominium? Is it located in the city, suburbs or in a rural area? Every structure has its own inherent pluses and minuses. That is simply how it is. What we want to do is identify those factors both positive and negative so that we can better assess how they may affect us.

What type of factors am I speaking of?

- *How large a residence is it?*
- *Does it have an area that could be used or is being used as a garden?*
- *What is the structure manufactured from?*
- *How are the utilities operated? Electricity, natural gas, propane, solar?*
- *How defensive a location is it?*
- *How old a structure is it?*

- *What weather conditions do I need to be aware of that might affect the structure?*
- *Where is it located? Urban, suburban or rural?*
- *How many people could you comfortably fit in it for an extended period if need be?*

Something I speak to people about often and, in particular my clients, is that if you are able to provide yourself the means to eat, stay hydrated and have shelter you can do the other things you need to do, build a better shelter, garden, stand security watch and so on. Just because you're situation is the way it is at any given point doesn't mean it has to stay that way.

What can we use as shelter? Here is a partial listing:

House	Apartment	Condominium
Camper	Automobile	Hotel/motel
Barn	Culvert	Tent
Debris Hut	Overpass	Cargo trailer
Railroad boxcar	Aircraft hanger	Garden shed
Storm cellar	Tunnels	Lean to

This listing is nowhere even remotely complete. Are there any on there that you hadn't thought about? How many more can you think of? The point being that your choices might be far more than what you thought they were.

Now in looking at the list are some of the options listed not you're first choice for shelter? Speaking for myself I can't say that having to live even for a short time in a culvert would not be much fun but if that is what I had to do until I could improve my situation, then so be it.

Each of the locations listed above would have its own special considerations to deal with. For example if you're stuck in your vehicle during a winter storm it would be advisable to run the vehicle periodically in order to run the heater but you would have to make sure to keep the exhaust pipe cleared to prevent buildup of carbon monoxide inside.

You would also want to not run it until it ran out of gas. That reduces your options considerably. Running the heater enough to keep you from freezing is very different than running it enough to make your comfortable. In a survival situation you do what you need to versus doing what you would like to. Another option to reduce the chance of freezing is to burn a single candle which can help raise the temperature several degrees. Caution must be taken to make sure that the candle doesn't start a fire especially with you in the vehicle!

Some may be wondering why there isn't a huge section in here on how to build a debris hut or an improvised lean to. Telling you how to do it isn't the same as you going out and learning how on your own. We must train and practice those skills we wish to know.

-o-

7 FIRE SAFETY

Fire safety is something that needs to be taken seriously, a good deal more seriously than just acknowledging the Public Service Announcements you invariably hear over and over during the holidays and usually ignore anyway. Fire deaths in the United States number in the thousands every year with hundreds of millions of dollars lost to fire damage. The sad fact of this is that most of the more than 1.5 million fires that occur in this country each year are preventable.

The United States still has a terrible problem with deaths due to fires, especially compared to other industrialized nations such as those found in parts of Europe and in Japan especially. In fact in Japan severe legal penalties often result if a fire is caused by negligence. This is a result of their deep seated cultural fear of fire. Throughout their history many devastating fires occurred as a result of their cities and towns being of basic wood construction and densely populated.

Fire is a necessary part of our everyday life. We use it to cook, dry our clothes; power our vehicles and much more. It is when we lose control of the beast that it turns on us. It can sweep through a house or office in a matter of a few short minutes. In the open, such as a grass fire or in a forest, fire can move faster than a person can run. In one instance I know of a grass fire in Nevada burned through 700 acres in less than one hour!

It is easier to understand the risks if we understand what we're talking about. So what is fire? Basically it is a chemical chain reaction involving four essential elements, all of which are need to keep the process going. The four elements that create fire are Fuel, it has to have something to burn; Oxygen, it needs to breath; Heat, the combustion starts here; and the fourth element required is a chemical reaction of the previous three. The removal of any of these four elements and the fire goes out. This is the fundamental concept of fire suppression.

What kinds of fire are there? Fires are divided into four classes based on the type of fuel involved.

CLASS A - Ordinary combustibles such as paper, wood, trash and textiles. Another way to remember this type is "A" for ash as all of these items will produce ash as it burns.

CLASS B – Flammable liquids such gasoline, kerosene, and oil. Use "B" for barrel as a way to remember since many liquids are stored in them.

CLASS C – Energized electrical equipment such as generators or electrical motors. Think "C" for current. Note, if the equipment is unplugged or in some other way it is no longer energized it is a Class A fire.

CLASS D – This is a special type of fire and rarely seen outside of industrial settings. This category includes such metals as titanium, sodium and magnesium. It requires a special type of fire extinguisher to quench this category of fire.

To combat the various Classes of fires there are a variety of extinguishers currently available:

DRY CHEMICAL – This is the most common one you will find. It can be used on Class A, B or C fires. It is also known as a multi-class. The agent is a dry powder which smothers the fire. It has a range of five to twenty feet. The vast majority of extinguishers sold for home protection are a dry chemical style.

FOAM – This creates a blanket of agent over the top of the fire both wetting the fuel and cutting off the oxygen keeping the fire from breathing. The key to use of this type of unit is that the agent must be arced or lobbed onto the fire. Spraying it directly onto the fire will not work effectively. This extinguisher is most effective against Class B fires, flammable liquids.

CO2 (carbon dioxide gas) -- Rarely seen these days but an effective extinguisher. The gas coming out of it is

VERY cold. One large drawback to this type of unit is its limited range, say no more than about eight feet. They also tend to empty quickly, especially compared to the dry chemicals units. Getting these units refilled is problematic as well.

The P.A.S.S. System

So you have never used a fire extinguisher? Don't let that intimidate you. It isn't as challenging as it might seem and I understand it can seem daunting. Each extinguisher is made up of several basic components common to nearly all types of extinguishers. The body, a hollow container which holds the extinguishing agent, a valve assembly, a nozzle and some have a hose assembly with the nozzle on the end of it. That's it.

A simple and easy to use acronym for using a fire extinguisher is P.A.S.S. It stands for

PULL – Remove the safety pin, this is usually secured to the top of the extinguisher to keep it from discharging accidentally.

AIM – Direct the discharge nozzle at the base of the fire.

SQUEEZE – Keeping the nozzle aimed at the base of the fire squeeze the handle to begin releasing the agent.

SWEEP – Move the discharge nozzle back and forth steadily across the base of the fire. Use the extinguisher in short spurts of 3-5 seconds each. This gives you more control and makes the agent in the extinguisher last longer.

Some Common Sense Guidelines About Fire Extinguishers

Fire extinguishers are there to allow you time to escape. They are NOT a primary means of fighting a large or even a medium size blaze.

Rule One: NEVER let the fire get between you and an exit while you're using the extinguisher.

Rule Two: If one extinguisher doesn't completely put the fire out it's time to leave. See Rule One above.

Even if you think the fire is out call the Fire Department. Fires can and will rekindle themselves more often than you think. The firefighters have the training, equipment, manpower and experience to deal with it. It is what they do. Your job is to stay alive. Things can be replaced -- you cannot.

Fire Safety Checklist

✓ Do not store gasoline, kerosene or other flammable liquids near heat sources or open flames.

✓ Do not overload electrical sockets, use multiple sockets instead of one with a multi outlet power strip.

✓ Extension cords are *temporary* wiring not a long term solution to power usage.

✓ Do not run electrical cords under rugs or carpet. They will wear, create bare spots and it will not be visible. These bare spots can come in contact with a flammable surface and start a fire.

✓ Have smoke detectors in your home and place of business. Change the batteries at least twice a year. A good time to remember to do it is at Daylight Savings. Change the clocks, change the batteries.

✓ Have a household evacuation plan in case of fire. Have an outside rally point for those in the home to go to after escaping so that you can quickly determine if everyone is out.

✓ During the holiday season if you are using a live Christmas tree keep it well watered. Make sure to clean up the dry needles from the tree and always make sure that there is no heat source near the tree. It is frightening how fast a dry Christmas tree can flash into a large flame fountain.

✓ Keep emergency numbers near the phone, not all areas have 911.

✓ Teach children to never play with matches, lighters or other open flame devices.

✓ Do not ever smoke in bed. You fall asleep with a lit cigarette and it can ignite the bedding.

✓ If you live in an area where wildfires are a risk, consider fire proof shingles for your home. Have a space of at least thirty (30) feet from your house clear of vegetation that can burn.

✓ Your roof should be made of metal, stucco, slate or composite materials. If you insist on using wood shingles, such as cedar shake, make sure they've been treated with a fire retardant.

✓ Your home siding should also be fire resistant. Metal, brick, stone and stucco are far better than a wooden exterior. If you have a wood exterior, make sure to treat it with fire retardants.

✓ Clean your roof and gutters of flammable debris, including leaves and pine needles.

✓ Remove any tree limbs within 10 feet of your chimney or stovepipe. Make sure flue openings are covered with small mesh or other protective grates.

✓ Landscaping should be spaced so that fire has no clear path to burn up to the house or nearby plantings. For a distance wide enough to prevent leaping embers from starting fires — perhaps 150 feet or so — make sure your ground is clear of dead trees and plants, the landscaping is well spaced and trees have been thinned out.

✓ Trim any tree branches up to 15 feet in height.

✓ A "fuel break" — devoid of any burnable material — should be maintained around any building on your property.

✓ Soak fireplace ashes or barbeque coals in water before disposing of them.

✓ Store gasoline only in an approved container and far from any occupied buildings. Keep propane tanks far from buildings and make sure the area around them is clear of flammable plant material.

✓ Any burnable material, including firewood, picnic tables and boats, should be kept away from all buildings.

✓ Keep your garden hose connected to the water spigot throughout fire season just in case and have it as long as possible. Bear in mind it is NOT a fire hose but can prove useful.

✓ All the roads to your property and your driveway should be at least 16 feet wide to allow emergency vehicles through. Make sure your house address is visible.

✓ Keep fire tools on the property: A ladder that can reach the roof, a sturdy shovel, a rake and a large water bucket all will help.

✓ Your home should have at least two entrances and exits.

Fire safety is an important aspect of daily life. Like so many other segments of preparedness it has to be practiced. Don't become complacent with your life and the lives of your family.

Consider having at least two multi-class extinguishers in your home. One near the kitchen is a good idea.

8 TO STAY OR TO GO

This can be one of the hardest decisions to make just prior to or immediately following things going bad. In some cases such as civil unrest or severe weather you will likely have at least some measure of advance warning but in other cases such as a terrorist attack or earthquake there may be no prior notice of the event occurring. The choices involved in staying or going will be many and complex. How serious is the problem that might force you to leave your home? How long could the problem last? Where are you going to go? What happens to your home if you do leave? Will you still have a job? And much more.

Bear in mind that depending upon the situation the choice to stay or go might not be up to you. If a mandatory evacuation is called for and enforced you will not have a choice of whether to leave or not. However you will have more options available to you if you have done the proper planning ahead of time by having a place to go. This could be the home of a friend or relative if you have a selection of goods, food and essentials ready to go. This means that you could be on the road well ahead of the masses allowing for quicker travel times and less hassles. Please note I said less hassles meaning there could still be issues you have to deal with such as lack of information, blocked roads, irate drivers and more.

Something to think about: how large is the population of the area in which you live? This could play a major role in whether or not you will need to leave right away or even at all. Despite the large land mass that the continental United States represents, a surprising amount of the population lives east of the Mississippi River. A huge number of those people live within an hour's drive of either the Atlantic Ocean or the Gulf of Mexico which means a significant number of people are highly localized in sprawling urban areas. These are the exact type of areas that will be extremely difficult to escape from if there is an urgent need to do so. Much the same is true of areas of the west coast, in particular southern California.

You need to pay attention to the routes that the population will likely follow. People, like water, will flow through the easiest channels first. These primary channels will be the interstate highways, but as more and more people try to leave an area the secondary and even tertiary roads will see their share of traffic. Frantic drivers, panicked by whatever the situation is, will cause accidents which will further clog these vital transportation arteries. Another concern is that these secondary roads are not designed for high traffic volume which means they will be easily fouled. This will hamper the egress causing drivers to seek other routes, anything to get away from where they were.

Most will not have a clue as to where they are trying to get to, just that they need to get away from where they were. Sadly this is not always the best plan at all. For many of these people staying at their residence, while not ideal, would be a much better idea than fleeing blindly "into the wilderness." Remaining at home is also known as "sheltering in place" and can mean that you are stuck at work. But at least you'd be indoors and with some measure of resources, however slim. Staying at home gives you even more options since it is your residence.

In many locations throughout the United States the interstate highways run right through the heart of major cities. This means that drivers could be forced to enter areas that are even more dangerous than the places they are leaving. Do not underestimate the viciousness of your fellow man, especially if the criminal element is deeply rooted in certain locations already. Exposing you and your family to attack is something to avoid always! Traveling with others who are like minded really helps -- in this case, there IS strength in numbers. One of the most nightmarish things to think about is that if the power is out then that means no working traffic lights -- further complicating the traffic problems, which may already be a gridlock situation or barely moving at best.

Another concern is trying to obtain fuel along the way. During the hurricane Katrina evacuations many people

---

reported that while they were pulled off alongside the roadways refueling their vehicles from gas cans that they were approached by others demanding that they share their gasoline. At times it was necessary for some of them to resort to a show of force, such as having more adults than those demanding the gas, or displaying firearms, to discourage the "requests."

Should you bring some fuel along with you if you are bugging out? I absolutely think you should but make sure it is stored properly and if possible out of sight of others. If you have to stop to refuel, get off the main road a bit, have security out and complete the refueling as quickly as possible. Then put the gas can back under cover. You know it's empty, but someone else won't and assume you have fuel.

Authorities could very well be totally overwhelmed by the scope of the mass migration; many of these same people will be trying to get their own families out and so will not be at work. This means that help, whether it is law enforcement, fire rescue, or medical may be limited at best and nonexistent at worst. How will you cope in this situation? Hopefully you will not ever have to deal with such a crisis but prior planning will reduce (not eliminate) your risks during this time. Now is the time to plan for something bad, not after it happens. Then you are not planning you are *reacting*, which is totally different.

Having a realistic and practiced plan ahead of time could mean the difference between not only living and dying but just scraping by or surviving and thriving. The key part of the previous sentence is "a realistic and practiced plan". You must establish your own criteria for what you feel the proper circumstances for staying or leaving are. That needs to be done at least in a planning manner ahead of time, like now for instance. What would make you stay, or what could come up that would force you to have to leave your home?

Holding up in your residence with 10,000 rounds of high power ammunition, a rifle, six freeze dried meals and two candles for light is not going to work. Neither would having six months worth of food if you have no way to safely cook it. It is crucial to be objective about your plans, your own experience and ability, the area in which you live and the threats you might actually face. It is all too easy to fall into the trap of believing that because you think a certain thing will happen a certain way that it will happen that way. That is also known as "wishful thinking."

One of the best ways to provide for yourself during a short-term situation is to have a 72 hour kit prepared ahead of time. For example, say a train derails a few blocks away and it becomes necessary for the authorities to order an immediate evacuation. You will NOT have the time to gather up all the supplies and goods you want/need. If you already have a kit packed you are going to be much better off than the vast majority of other people. After all, isn't that what we've been talking about?

Food – Enough for two heavy meals per person per day for the three days and some way to prepare it safely. Heavy meals since you might be stressed and the body needs more fuel to keep itself operating more efficiently during those times.

Water – No less than a gallon per person per day at the barest minimum but three gallons a day is better. Having a small, quality water filter would be a great way to handle this.

Clothing – At least two changes of clothes per person including a pair of quality shoes.

Medical – A good first aid kit as well as a stock of any prescription medications.

Paperwork – Copies of all your vital records such as birth certificates, shot records, current maps, etc.

Money – Have enough cash to cover fuel, food and if need be hotel room rental for at least the 72 hours. Do NOT expect credit cards and checks to be accepted.

Toiletries – Soap, shampoo, toothpaste, toothbrush, deodorant etc.

Miscellaneous – Matches, a flashlight, a deck of cards, a multi-tool such as a Leatherman, another thing to bring along is a small am/fm radio, solar charger for cell phone.

All of these goods can fit inside a pair of large plastic storage tubs (two 55 gallon size or three 33 gallon size) which is then easily transported from the residence to your vehicle and away you go. Another choice are sturdy backpacks. Note this is not the same as a BOB (Bug Out Bag)

since a BOB may not have enough for a 72 hour period.
Could your BOB suffice in this role? Yes it could if it is
properly packed. But bear in mind that a BOB is designed to
be worn so if you are going to pack it heavy then get out and
train yourself by regularly wearing it while walking for
distance. The other advantage is you get in some good
exercise which is nothing but a plus for you.

Stay or Go?

To better understand the issues involved with staying
or going let's take a look at some pros and cons of both.
These lists are based on a situation that allows you the
choice of staying or going at your discretion.

Staying

PRO	CON
More options at your home	Martial Law in area
Familiar with your surroundings	Damage to structure depending on event
Having neighbors around	Not enough manpower
Less restrictions	Looters
Like minded people coming to you	Not having a place to go
Fuel on-hand going for other uses	People draining your resources

Going

PRO	CON
Getting out of a danger area	Having enough fuel to leave danger area
Having a pre-determined destination	Not having a certain destination
You control if and when you leave	Ending up in a shelter without choices
Like minded people to travel with	No like minded people around
Having more options than some others	Vehicle size limits what you can bring

There are obviously a number of pluses and minuses that could go in both areas but I wanted to highlight some of the more essential information regarding this. Each person and their situation will be the driving force behind the choice to stay or go. It requires a look at the history of an area -- does it suffer severe weather such as hurricanes on a regular basis? Is there a track record of earthquakes? Is the area vulnerable to power outages which would mean no municipal water? It pays to do your homework in this area.

A big consideration about going is having a place to go to. I've touched on it a few times so let's take a better look at that. If your plan is to "head for the hills" as many people say they will, what is your plan once you get to "the hills"?

Where will you stay? Obtain clean water? Procure food and cook it? Think you will suddenly become a hunter and be able to put meat on the table on a regular basis? Don't try -- it won't work for long. You will either hunt the area out of edible game or the combination of you and whoever else headed for the hills will. That is of course assuming that there was game in the area in the first place. If you have a pre-arranged destination, that is different -- a friend's house or maybe it's grandma's place out in the country.

If you don't have a place to go then you could end up in a relocation center or other type of officially operated shelter. One of the down sides to this is that you may (I want to emphasize the may, meaning it might not be this way) be told that you need to surrender your goods, any and all weapons, food etc. That means you will rely on someone else to tell you when, what and if you can eat, where and when you can sleep or shower. Not a pleasant situation. I understand that the people operating the shelters are doing the best they can but in a large scale situation the sheer numbers of those that need assistance can easily overwhelm resources. Vast numbers of people being displaced means that they create traffic, demands for food, ice, fuel, medical care and information.

Part of having a place to go is making sure you can get there. Drive the routes that will take you to where you are planning to go ahead of time. Routes, plural, meaning more than one. Most places can be reached by more than the direct way. Get off the interstate and take the state highway that loops around from the west side or take side streets to get your buddy's house.

Don't get locked in on the thought that there is only one way to get someplace. By driving the various routes ahead of time you will have some familiarity with the drive. Make the drive for a reason, use it as a means to pre-position two or three tubs worth of food, clothes and supplies at your destination. If you absolutely have to leave with little more than the clothes on your back then something is waiting for you. If you have enough time to pack and/or grab your 72 hour kit then you have even more on-hand when you arrive. Remember living a preparedness lifestyle is about increasing the number of options you have.

-o-

9 ENTRY GOODS

What in the world are we talking about here? What the term "entry goods" means in this context are the supplies and equipment that either you would bring to someone else's house or that you would want someone to bring with them if they are coming to your home in the time of an emergency/crisis.

Why is having this list of goods necessary? Think of it in these terms, six of your relatives showed up at 2 a.m. after driving for two days to escape a hurricane or earthquake. Do you have enough on-hand to feed all of them and you for a week or two? What about bedding, what about toilet paper?

Don't say it can't happen. During the Katrina situation numerous people suddenly found themselves with house guests, family, friends and even friends of friends. Many of these had little more than the clothes on their back or what little they could stuff in their vehicles, which in many cases was the "wrong" stuff. In many cases their "visitors" turned into long term house guests who strained resources and relationships, some beyond repair.

If these same guests had brought goods with them, or pre-positioned a load at your residence, it could take a huge strain off of *your* resources. Remember we are talking about supplies that *you* paid for, not them.

So having explained this concept a bit, what goes into planning this? Here is a sample listing of what I, as well as a large number of folks I know, use as starting point for building their list. I have goods and foods belonging to others placed at my house for their use if the need arises and I have goods located with friends as well. I want to stress that the amount here are suggestions and not absolutes so feel free to start with smaller amounts, at least in regards to food.

The List

30 days of food stuffs, totaling no less than 90 servings (food amount is **per** person)

4 complete changes of clothing, including footwear and such

2 complete change of bedding; (sleeping bag and blanket/pillow)

Personal hygiene items

Complete set of eating utensils per person

10 rolls of toilet paper

5 rolls of paper towels

2 containers of laundry soap

1 gallon of dish soap

1 Gallon of hand soap

Some means of pest control (mouse traps or roach traps, etc)

20 gallons of gasoline aside from what is in the vehicle(s)

10 gallons of transportable water

5 gallons of transportable diesel

Basic First Aid Kit

Communications gear of a common type such FRS, HAM or GMRS radios

Spare batteries for electronics

Basic tool kit including pioneer tools (shovel, pick, etc)

Paracord (min 100 ft)

Duct Tape (minimum 3 rolls)

Trash bags (55 gallon contractor grade)

1 main rifle, of common military caliber or the equivalent

1000 rounds of ammo for the above rifle

1 sidearm of defensive caliber, 500 rounds of ammo for above pistol

1 weapon cleaning kit

1 special caliber weapon (shotgun or .22), minimum 500 rounds for this weapon

Shelter item such as tent and tarp

Optional Items to consider bringing or storing in place:

Cooking utensils

High lift bumper jack

High strength tow strap or chain

Manual come-along winch

Holster/ cases for firearms

High quality footwear

Candles, lanterns or lamps

Morale items (games, books, cards, etc)

Educational material for children

Binoculars

Propane (either one pound cans or the larger 25# unit)

Now, you have looked at this list and said to yourself, no way, is he kidding me??? I can't possibly get all that stuff bought, packed up and transported...Stop for moment and relax, there are ways to "cheat" to further reduce the transportation issue.

The bulkiest part of the list is the food, 30 days of food for one person is a good amount I grant you but this is where the "cheating" comes in. Don't think of it as cheating, think of it instead as smart planning. This entire list will fit in a stack of plastic tubs which is how you should try to move it for sake of storage space and convenience.

So how do you do all this? Actually you **don't** carry it all when you are trying to leave. A great rule of thumb in regards to entry goods and bugging out is the 50/25/25 rule. If you have never heard of it goes like this:

50% of your goods at your main residence

25% of your goods stored at what you are going to

25% of your goods pre-loaded for transport

Total: 100% of your goods

Pre-position? Where do I do that at? This is one of the more difficult issues facing those who will at some point potentially need to bug out. This is mainly due to trust and that is a hard commodity to find at times. Who do you trust enough to help ensure the lives and safety of you and your family? Does that clear that issue up a bit? Because this is what we are talking about, the safety and survival of you and your family.

Think about where you are right now and then think about who you know that lives a reasonable distance from you. Family and friends that are just far enough away to make it hard to get to in a reasonable drive during non emergency times are the perfect distance. It is worth considering that if the event forcing you to leave covers a wide enough area it might affect them too but if you used the threat checklist at the beginning of the book you will know this already.

Having success in being prepared requires prior planning. The formula above is completely adjustable. For example if you don't have a large vehicle capable of hauling the 25% then increase the amount of material you have at the destination making it easier and less stressful on you if you are forced to leave.

So, let's take a look at some of the questions that need answers for this to work:

So how do I pre-position goods? That is actually one of the easiest fixes. The use of inexpensive (low priced NOT low quality, cheap junk) stackable storage tubs with tight fitting lids is a winning strategy. They are easy to handle, stackable and uniform size making them my number one choice for storage containers. Now, having sung their praises, are they perfect? No, if the lids are not on properly, rodents can get in (had this happen in our camping gear, my own fault, lids were not tight). But for the money, the convenience and the utility of these are, in my opinion, your best option.

What do I store at this other location? Ideally, the larger items that take up bulk and are the heaviest. Food, fuel and ammunition immediately come to mind. Read the list again, 30 days of food *per* person is a large amount. Now another way to "cheat" is to store a week's worth to start out, costs less and it is still adding to your level of safety.

There is now food there for you, then as you can add to what is being stored. Does it mean that you have to buy the stuff, transport it and all that? No, one thing that some folks I know do is send a shopping list and a check to the people they intend to shelter with. The folks on the other end buy the goods and add it to the pre-positioned supplies. No transportation costs and it saves time which could be critical if you are forced to leave your primary location because you don't have to load food.

For some the question of why you would want/need weapons is there as well. That is an individual choice based on your own attitude toward self defense, your local laws regarding firearm ownership and your own level of commitment to survival. I have spoken with a number of individuals who went through the Katrina hurricane event, those who evacuated by use of their own vehicles, those who had family members and friends come to stay with them as a result of evacuating. I also have a good friend who worked high profile armed security in the gulf region for a number of months following Katrina and Rita.

Something that became apparent in many of these conversations was that those that had firearms were more secure. Their stress levels, while still high, were not as high as those without the means to protect themselves. Some of those traveling in groups by vehicle set up security around the vehicles when they were stopped. Others found it necessary to have firearms around while they were refueling by the side of the road due to aggressive approaches by others demanding that they share their gasoline. So again the choice of having firearms is entirely up to you -- but for me it is being armed.

Now when it comes to weapons I would NOT recommend pre-positioning firearms. Ammunition, no problem, but not the guns themselves. Short of buying a gun safe for your home and another for there as well, how would you guarantee the security of the weapons? Remember this is a pretty heavy financial investment you are making in buying firearms. Plus, if you have to travel, don't you want the weapons with you?

-o-

Another key to this issue is practicing. You have to get out and make the investment in time and effort now before a situation arises that might force you to leave. Wouldn't it be nice to be able to pack up exactly what you need and be out the door in an hour or less? While everyone else is running around going "Oh crap, where is the damned tent, where are the flashlights, where is this, where is that?" you are already on the road ahead of a good portion of the throng that *will* be clogging up the roads in short order.

Imagine having a full thirty minutes head start on 80+% of the exodus. This is, of course, only if things are so bad you must evacuate. Often times, in fact most of the time, sheltering in place is likely your best option.

Having a current checklist already printed out of what items to bring is a great time saver. If you have to leave then the stress factor will be high already. Compound that by trying to remember what to bring is a headache worth avoiding. If things are so bad that you have to leave then the "oh sh*t" factor will be in full force. Better to have a pre-written list of what to grab to reduce your chances of forgetting something that you will need later.

By practicing you know what works, what doesn't, where things are and what you can *realistically* carry in your vehicle(s). One of the things you have to bear in mind when packing is weight. Gasoline, water and the other liquids are *heavy*, so having as much of the other supplies already placed where you are going will be a huge factor in your favor. The average automobile in use in this country will **not** be able to carry 1500 pounds of supplies. Do the math, take the list and figure out the weight of it and you will see that it quickly adds up. I know for my family of five, a 30 day entry goods weighed in at over 2000 pounds. That's right, a full ton, and that wasn't counting the weight of the people. That is a serious amount of weight to try and move.

Preparedness is about having options, back ups for your back ups is a phrase that floats around in the preparedness minded community because it is true. At the beginning of the book I told you that there is no one thing that will ensure your safety. This is part of that; it is the process that improves your chances. The more options you have the better your chances.

By pre-positioning a portion of your supplies you can maximize your options while reducing your risk factors. Note that I said "reducing" not "eliminating." Think those thousands of people who had to endure the conditions in the Louisiana Super Dome immediately following Katrina wouldn't have given their eye tooth and then some to have another choice? Think their attitude toward prepping has changed? Sad to say, for some of them and many others following an event, it still doesn't wake them up. Others get the idea and start making the changes to keep it from happening to them. Experience can be a harsh teacher, if a trifle short tempered at times.

It really comes down to how much do you want to avoid being a refugee. Having someone else dictate to you when and where you can sleep, what, when or if you can eat, when, where, how and if you travel. How much of YOUR belongings you get to keep? Not me friends, not me. So having some of your goods along with you as well as some at your destination are other ways of reducing the chances of this happening. It is about a system, a mindset of saying to yourself, *this is what I have to do to survive and I am going to do it.*

So start looking around for those you trust, and I mean really trust. This is your life and the lives of your family we are talking about. Feeling uneasy yet? Feeling like you know you need to do something but it seems overwhelming? Remember, preparedness is NOT something that can be fixed in a day, a weekend, or a week for most of us. It is a lifestyle change and for that to happen you have to be consistent at it. Every week you do a bit more and a bit more, first you get more food and then you store and treat an extra ten gallons of gas, you get out the camping gear and make sure it is in good shape, you replace the batteries in the flashlights like you've been meaning to for some time…

Something that we did was whenever we got

something like the things above done, we wrote it down. It was our way of tracking our progress; we knew that every time we added something to the list we were a little better off. Or if you prefer, write out a list of all the things you feel you need to do and then cross them off as you get them done. It is a great psychological boost either way. It keeps you energized and that always helps. It helps because there will be days that you ask yourself, *Why the hell am I doing this? What is the point?*

When that happens and like I said, it will, just stop and take a look around. Go watch your kids doing their homework or while they are playing and then ask yourself what are you going to do to keep them from being cold, wet or hungry. It always worked for me. Everyone's motivation is different and you have to find what works for you, but it is there.

So you work out ahead of time where you are going and get with that person. Maybe work out an exchange system, you store things at their house and they do it at yours. After all, how much space are we talking about? A lot less than what you think. Two stacks of say five tubs each in the garage or in the basement. Do you realize how much you could actually store in those ten tubs? It is a good deal more than what you might think. Properly stored those ten tubs could easily hold the food for four people for at least a week, clothes, some fuel, candles, flashlights, some tools, ammunition and more.

The key is taking the time to do the packing properly. Put the clothes in oversize plastic bags to protect them from insects and rodents. Put only canned food in the tubs, especially since this is what weighs the most of your food and it will store longer if kept in a cool environment. A basic tool kit is not expensive at all. The same is true of lanterns and candles. One surplus military ammunition can, readily available and inexpensive, could easily hold a variety of ammunition and stores easily.

Plan ahead and then DO! Entry Goods do work so take advantage of the hard won experience of others and put it to use.

-o-

10 BUG OUT BAG

This particular item has a selection of names depending upon who you ask. The B.O.B. or Bug Out Bug, the Bug Home Bag, the Emergency Bag, Go Bag...you get the idea. The important thing is to understand what its purpose is, and then put however many you need for your family together. After that you can pick your own name for it! Sound good to you?

When "survivalism" was becoming more popular back in the '70's one of the notions being put forward back then was the idea of *Backpack Survivalism*. It involves slinging a well stuffed backpack over your shoulders and "heading for the hills" to try and survive.

Can you imagine trying to carry what you need with you and only having what you can carry with you? I genuinely believe that backpack survivalism will not work for the overwhelming majority of the people. There are certainly hardcore hikers and outdoor types that have the experience and skills that they could survive using this method -- but the underlying question is for how long?

If there is game in the area it will be quickly hunted out. Even then when people are lucky enough to secure their prize, do they have the skill to process it so that most of the meat doesn't go to waste? Water sources could easily become contaminated leading to illness, or even death if the case is severe enough. What about shelter? Think someone has a portable log cabin they can tote around?

If any of that seems harsh I'm not going to apologize. The scorn was deliberate. We are not an outdoor living society. Hardship and lack of comfort is not something that we Americans tend to deal with well. Sadly, following an event that is exactly what we end up dealing with. For some it is more than they can handle.

Having a "go bag" is a personal choice but it's one that I personally believe very strongly in. My bag stays in my truck unless I am going to be away from home with someone else in their car, then it goes with me. Some of the benefits of having supplies with you include peace of mind, ability to treat injury, having food and water, having a change of clothes and to the ability to generate fire. Overall a pretty good list I think.

Do yourself a huge favor and don't go the cheap route when choosing a bag, get a quality bag. If you are ever in a situation that you need what is in the bag, don't cheat yourself and go the low dollar route. These supplies could literally save your life.

In my case I have to be careful with the overall weight of the bag as not to overtax my shoulder. My left shoulder is artificial due to a line of duty injury when I was a firefighter so I am limited to about 35 pounds total. This makes my BOB choices all the more critical. Here is what I have in my bag:

MEDICAL KIT

2 Pair of large vinyl medical gloves	Disposable CPR mask
2 triangular bandages	2 disposable foil blankets
1 pair shears	1 roll 2" medical tape
10 packets antibiotic ointment	3 packets burn gel
10 packets sting relief wipe	4 acetominophen/ibuprofen caplets
10 packets iodine prep wash	5 packets Germ X wipes
6 anti-diarrhea tablets	6 Pepto Bismol Tablets
10 butterfly-style bandages	5 ¾"x3" bandaids
5 large patch bandaids	5 knuckle bandaids
5 fingertip bandaids	8 sterile 4x4 pads

| 1 5x9 sterile trauma pad | 2 gauze rolls, 2" wide |
| 1 8x10 sterile trauma pad | 2 sterile gauze rolls, 4" wide |

FOOD / WATER

2 Complete MREs (Meals Ready to Eat)

2 700 ML Reusable Water Bottles

Assorted energy bars and electrolyte replacements packets

CLOTHING

1 Bandana, 1 Pair of socks

HYGIENE

1 toothbrush, 1 small toothpaste, 1 small liquid soap, 1 package cough drops, 1 roll toilet paper

MISCELLANEOUS

1 elastic camouflage cover, 1 map of Oklahoma, 1 compass, 1 pair binoculars, 1 Leatherman style multi-tool, 1 backstrap strap, 50 strike anywhere matches, 1 pair 72" bootlaces, and 5 assorted chemical lightsticks.

-o-

Some thoughts on this list: As the seasons change I add or remove items as necessary. For example, in the fall I add more clothing such as a thermal undershirt and change out the socks for a heavier wool pair. I check the bag over for wear and the contents for conditions. One of the biggest things I do is to put the pack on and wear it around to keep myself acclimated to the feel of it. If you don't exercise regularly you can't expect to be able to just grab your bag and then walk the 8.7 miles home with it on your back if your vehicle dies or the roads become impassable. You must train with your equipment. After all, we are talking about potentially saving your life. Isn't that worth the time and effort?

The list above like so many of them in this book is not intended to be an absolute. It is provided to give you a starting point. Everyone's situation is unique and so their planning needs to reflect that.

For example if the person is a smaller frame female their physical ability will differ from that of a 6'2" man which is simply the reality of the differences. She may be able to better hike the distance with a load than he is. It comes down to willpower as well.

Living a preparedness lifestyle means you have to make the investment in a large number of areas to improve your overall situation which is exactly what we are trying to do. Your health, the networking that you do, the amount of exercise you commit to, building up and maintaining of food stocks and more. The BOB is the same, you need to work at coming up with what is best for you and your situation.

On the next page are some additional items that you may consider having in your BOB.

Single burner stove	A book	A small tent
Complete change of clothes	A signal mirror	Notepad
Pens/pencils	Currency/coins	Junk silver coins
Firearm/ammunition	Freeze dried food	Poncho

Again this is just a partial listing, be creative and embrace the concept of being able to survive on the go. Stay safe.

-o-

11 VEHICLES

The choice of the proper vehicle can play a significant role in your preparedness plans. Having the right vehicle for the situation could mean the difference in being able to accomplish your goal. Now, before I go deeper into this I want to make it clear that I am **not** advocating you run out and buying a new(er) vehicle simply to have on-hand as a BOV (Bug Out Vehicle).

I understand that times are hard and many readers are working at or near their financial limits as it is. Besides, in the Budget chapter I talked about reducing your debt so going out and getting another vehicle is hardly reducing your debt. What I am talking about here is providing you the information on vehicles much like I am doing throughout the book on other topics. Size, weight capacities, towing and much more to help provide you the information to make a more informed decision when the time is right for you.

What are some of the more desirable characteristics we might want to consider in a vehicle for a preparedness minded person?

CAPABILITY	BENEFIT
Reasonably high ground clearance	Allows access to more terrain areas
Larger gas tank capacity	More driving distance available
Towing capability	Able to pull some manner of external load
Larger passenger capacity	Able to carry more people / cargo

I honestly don't believe that there is a perfect criterion for selecting a vehicle due to the many differences in both geographic and demographic factors. What works for a small family in Nevada may be totally wrong for a large family in upstate Maine. A vehicle decision has to include choice about the terrain and weather of an area, as well as the size and makeup of the people using it. The items I listed above are my own recommendations for desirable options in a vehicle, not absolutes.

In my case I own a full size four wheel drive pick-up truck. It has dual fuel tanks, shock absorbers suited for off road travel, decent ground clearance, good towing capability as well as sizable cargo capacity. Having said all that is it ideal? No, it only has room for three passengers in the cab and despite the twin fuel tanks it doesn't get especially great gas mileage -- much of my sizable cargo capacity would be eaten up by the necessity of carrying extra fuel cans.

Don't get me wrong the truck is much more useful that many others vehicles for a number of reasons but it isn't for everyone. The point I'm making is that a good hard, objective look at your own situation is called for in regards to selecting the best balance among the options available in vehicles.

An important fact to be aware of is that the typical sedan in use in the United States today is NOT well suited to handle large amounts of cargo or extensive off road driving. The reason I want to bring this up is to ensure that if you have a vehicle along those lines you are aware of that fact. Does it mean that the vehicle is useless? Of course not, however it could very well mean that you will have to do a highly prioritized loading to use what capabilities the vehicle does have.

My pickup truck

Vehicle Maintenance

No matter what vehicle you drive you should ensure that it is in the best possible mechanical shape. Tires properly inflated and rotated if/when required, oil changed on a regular basis, essential fluids kept topped off and the engine tuned up. Not only does this mean that if something happens your vehicle is more likely to be able handle some hard driving but it helps to protect the investment in the vehicle as well, which helps its resale value. Another factor regarding upkeep is that it is less likely to break down -- saving you money and inconvenience as well. So keeping a vehicle in proper form is a win-win for you.

If you have the proper skill to perform your own regular maintenance, fantastic! Not everyone has the ability or equipment to do this. If you have to take your vehicle somewhere for service, make sure it is a quality firm with certified mechanics. Check with your friends and co-workers to see where they take their vehicles, ask at the local Chamber of Commerce for tips on good businesses also. It is too important not to have the work done correctly.

Right now I want to bring up some vehicle issues so we can take a look at them.

- *Do you know where in your vehicle the spare tire is? Is it a regular or donut style?*
- *Do you know how to properly change a tire? Have you ever done it? Do you have the jack and other equipment accessible for a rapid tire change?*
- *Know how to check the oil and other fluids? (antifreeze, brake fluid, power steering, transmission)*

If not then learn, learn by doing. Put on some older clothes, go out and change your own tire. Better that, than trying to learn how to do it on the side of the road, at night, in the rain. Have the mechanic at the shop teach you where to put the oil in the engine. It could be that you might be the only help you have available if there is a problem.

Another benefit is that helps builds confidence in yourself, knowing that you are more capable of dealing with potential emergencies. Buy and keep in the car a good quality book on that particular vehicle make and model. These are available at nearly all of the larger auto part stores for under $20. A good investment.

What To Have In Your Vehicle?

This can be a difficult question since it falls into the "what works best for you" category. So here is listing of some goods and supplies I recommend that you keep in your vehicle(s) just in case.

Motor oil (1 quart)
Jumper cables
Flares
Fire extinguisher (ABC capable)
Water (1 gallon)
Anti Freeze (1 gallon)
Tool kit
Blanket
Emergency Triangle (to alert other cars)
First Aid kit
Fully functional spare tire
Proper jack and lug wrench

Current map / atlas showing your area
Some cash (emergency tows, food, etc)
Food (at least six meals worth for one)
Flashlight with spare batteries
Tow chains / straps
Shovel (a small folding unit will work)

These items (except the spare tire) could fit in a large plastic tub in the trunk or rear cargo area depending upon the type of vehicle it is. This saves you room as well as making it easier to find what you need when you really need it. If you have a pick-up truck, consider adding a cross bed locking tool box. You would still have the space underneath the box for cargo and it gives you storage space for a wide variety of the equipment above. If you don't currently have all these items prioritize the purchases just as you would other prep buying and get them.

Again we are talking about increasing your options so keep your vehicle(s) in good working order with the proper supplies onboard. Safe driving!

-0-

12 THE BUG OUT TRAILER

One of the terms that you may have already run across at some point is B.O.T. which stands for Bug Out Trailer -- also the name of this cleverly titled chapter. In the Vehicle chapter we talked about the issue of transporting the supplies and equipment you will need. A B.O.T. is another way of doing that, which further improves your options.

A quick word of caution: some of the issues we discussed earlier in the book regarding many of the vehicles available today to the general public such as cargo room and weight handling capability are still in play, but I'm going to add a further one -- towing capacity. Some vehicles have excellent towing capacity while others won't tow a kiddie wagon. In the rush toward higher fuel economy, during the last decade in particular, one aspect of vehicle performance that has been sacrificed is the ability to tow something. For example a friend of mine has a SUV with a hybrid engine and it gets great mileage, is roomy and comfortable. But it is totally incapable of towing anything per the manufacturer! By contrast my 1985 Chevy pickup will tow quite a bit but doesn't get anything remotely resembling great mileage. So there is a trade off, no question.

So is having a B.O.T. the right thing for you? Hard to answer since everyone's situation is unique to them. There are a large number of factors to consider among these are, in no particular order:

- *Is my vehicle capable of towing a trailer safely?*

- *What is my plan? Do I have a legitimate need for a trailer?*

- *Where will the trailer be kept? Do I have the room for it?*

- *What is the cost of the unit?*

- *Will it need to be insured?*

- *What is my planned evacuation route if I do have to leave? (Ground clearance concerns)*

- *If I am leaving do I have a place to go to?*

- *Would having the bulk of my supplies pre-positioned be a better plan?*

- *How much am I planning on taking with me if I must go? Size, weight?*

- *Would having a trailer be valuable to me for other uses and still work as a BOT?*

- *Would having a BOT at my home compromise my OPSEC?*

- *If I have a trailer hitch on my vehicle is it adequate to haul a well loaded trailer?*

- *What (if any) upgrades might I need to think about to the vehicle? (transmission cooler, etc.)*

- *I already have a camper trailer, won't that work?*

- *If I have to go then I'll just go rent a trailer somewhere, that will work won't it?*

Seems like an awful long list and to be honest it is. Having a B.O.T. is not for everyone and that fact needs to be stated plainly. Do I have one currently? No, I do not. Have I owned one in the past? Yes, I did. My personal situation changed so my prep plans had to be adjusted. One of the greatest strengths of a preparedness lifestyle is its flexibility.

I am currently living at my B.O.L. or Bug Out Location if you will. It is a go to place for several other families who all have some goods pre-positioned here. Each family is also planning on, and quite honestly, is expected to bring much more with them if it ever becomes necessary for them to bug out. There are several trailers here at the farm that could be pressed into service quite easily for use as a B.O.T. if the need should arise.

I'd like to take a specific look at two of the questions from the list and address them here. The last two questions were put there on purpose. Having a camper trailer could definitely work for use as a B.O.T. if it was matched up with the right tow vehicle and there is adequate space for the additional supplies and equipment. A camper trailer also gives you another large feature and that of course is shelter. You are bringing the means to keep you out of the elements with you and that is not a small advantage.

One thing to remember is that in many cases there are existing supplies and equipment that will serve you in a dual capacity, such as camping gear. Having "stuff" that serves you in more than one way does nothing but help you. When I was married my wife and I loved taking the family camping. We did it several times a year which also allowed us the opportunity to tweak our equipment as needed based on real world usage.

The final question on the list talked about simply running out and renting a trailer when you needed to. In my opinion there are several significant problems that could arise with that plan but here are my main two.

What if you can't get a trailer because they are all gone already or otherwise unavailable? So now you only have the ability to move a small portion of what you want to bring with. How would you prioritize what you have to leave behind? You've also lost valuable time in trying to acquire the trailer.

If you wait to get a trailer then have to load it you'll likely be caught in the mass exodus. Any chance of getting out ahead of the hordes that WILL clog the roads is now gone. You and your family could be stuck in a massive traffic jam for hours, or worse indefinitely, with no ability to make progress toward your destination.

A concept I "may" have touched on in other areas of the book is to make sure you practice with your equipment and that absolutely includes practicing a load out of the goods and supplies you plan on bringing with you. I was with a large preparedness group on the west coast for several years and we got in the habit of at least once a year doing a full load out.

Following the first one we did an After Action Report on it in which everyone was asked to share their individual stories of how it went. In particular we were all asked to make a list of three things that went right, three things that didn't do well and what was the total time it took to load out. One rule that we all agreed to prior to starting was that we had to load the actual goods, no substituting empty tubs or boxes for the real thing.

For my part I was truly caught off guard when I realized that between my wife's minivan and my full size pickup that we didn't have enough room for the five of us and all the goods we had intended to bring. It also took a good deal longer to load up than we had thought it would in spite of the fact that much of our gear was pre-packed and ready to go. For the rest of the group it was a mix of results as well.

Among the things that went well was having a checklist of what to grab. Not having a checklist proved to be a major problem for several members. Universally it was discovered that loading out took longer than just about everyone anticipated including those who did have a checklist. We made the drill a yearly event and it was a huge help to the group and its members. So, if you do have or plan to get a B.O.T., practice with it.

-o-

13 NETWORKING

What is it and why do I need it? Well networking is just what the name suggests, establishing and maintaining a link with others who are like minded *and* who are actively preparing. (Let me clarify something: the previous sentence is MY criteria for networking, some people are fine with hooking up with folks who are just like minded.)

Why do I have both criteria in my definition? For me it's an easy question to answer. Why would you try to link up with those who are not of the same mind set and not actively working on improving their situation? You don't because they will only be a drain on *your* resources which are already committed to providing for you and yours.

Resources following an event, especially if it is a severe one and/or covers a large geographic area may be scarce to non-existent depending on circumstances. What you have on-hand might be it, the sum of what you have to survive on for an extended period. Why have someone else with you who is only draining those resources with little to nothing for you to gain in return? Simply because he is a nice guy or you are? Sorry, that is not nearly a good enough reason for me. Not when it is a choice between them and me.

Remember, the preparedness lifestyle at its core is about the safety of your family. Networking is another way of increasing your options. Since you're either currently expending time, energy and money on preparedness or planning to, doesn't it make sense to do it working with those who are doing the same? You learn from them, they learn from you. How much is it worth to you to have someone telling you not to buy a certain brand or type of equipment because they did and it was a piece of junk? You can consolidate your money with others (in the right situation) to buy in bulk so that everyone saves money.

Does what I am telling you mean you can't talk to your neighbor Ray who is a good friend but refuses to prep? Of course not, but searching out and finding others who feel as you do is something that you must do if you want to not only survive but survive and thrive. There is a world of difference between the two.

I'm going to warn you in advance it isn't easy at times especially when you are first moving into this phase of prepping. There is no great national preparedness test given to our citizens (oh how I wish!) which is then graded and the results sent out. Chances are if you take a careful look around you might already know folks who are quietly into preparedness. Parents, grandparents (<u>never</u> overlook resources), friends, acquaintances from church or work, fellow members of civic groups, local faith based community organizations, Red Cross chapters and yes, internet sources.

A few words on that last one. The internet is an amazing place full of information, some good and some terrible, entertainment and fascinating people. It also unfortunately has its share of liars, thieves and predators. Tread wary when dealing with people online. People can say they are anyone while online which is how many children are enticed away from homes and schools to meet their "friend" which can lead to abuse or worse.

One very tried and proven method of dealing with folks via the internet is to do it slowly. Use the different search engines to look for preparedness groups, forums, etc. Visit these sites as much as you can (a list of some of these may be found in the back of this book in the Resources section). Once you have found one or two you like focus you attention on those. If you are paying attention you will see who posts often, who posts good information and who is a manure spreader (there are LOTS and LOTS of those). Be cynical about what you read and see there. Avoid those who like to throw around phrases such as "well I think this should work" or the "this is what I heard" types. If they themselves are not out there doing it, actually putting action to their plans, avoid them. Begin to talk to those that seem to have their act together.

Take your time; establish a regular e-mail correspondence with them. Be ever so slow in giving out vital details of your personal life to them. The next step is usually exchanging phone calls with many folks preferring to give out their cell numbers rather than their house number. Then after all that if you feel comfortable with it set up a meeting in a mutually agreed on neutral spot like a city park, library or restaurant. Then you can really start the process of getting to know them. If they are the genuine article then the security steps will not deter them. It is only through demonstration that you can really start to get a handle on who a person really is and they can see the type of person you are.

Do they follow up and do what they say they are going to? Is their work ethic a good one? How do they treat their children and yours? It is through their actions, not just their words that they need to be judged on. Can they be counted on to be were they said they would when they said they would be there? Are they drinkers or smokers? The reason for the last question is if there is a disruption in the normal ability to restock those items it could lead to inter-personal issues. Every seen a drinker or smoker go through withdrawals? Not pretty to watch.

I could tell you of a number of true stories about those that I know and are acquainted with that have benefited from being properly networked. Stories of how folks showed up following an east coast hurricane to assist. This help driving in from three states away paying the costs out of their own pocket to help cut up downed trees, repair homes and such simply because a forum member asked. Or how a group of like minded friends gave up time while on a camping trip because they found out that another member who lived nearby was in need of help clearing up some storm damage. This same member had a number of family in the area that he had on many occasions helped out and none of them were willing to come over when *he* really needed it.

The reason that this occurred was because the members of this particular group had taken the time to get to know each other, and to prove themselves worthy of trust and respect. My daughter was visiting friends in a state some distance from home. I sent one of the members in that area I had dealt with previously an email asking if it would be alright to give my daughter their contact information just in case. He immediately replied yes and supplied me with a whole series of phone numbers for him, his work, his wife, etc. Fortunately it turned out not to be needed but I can't tell you how much better I felt knowing that my daughter had reliable help a phone call away.

At that time I hadn't met this man in person but through interaction via the forum with him and seeing how he treated others I was comfortable with him. Networking is a very important part of life; you do it now with your job and in your home life. You talk to friends to find out who a reliable mechanic is, to seek out competent legal help, find the best place for groceries and more. So all you are doing in regards to preparedness is focusing your questions.

Once again let me caution you about giving away information regarding your preparedness plans. I don't believe I can overstate the importance of maintaining a low profile in regards to this. Word of mouth travels much,

much further than you might imagine. Caution and awareness will serve you well in this search. You don't want to be associated with someone who just says they do this or that, if they aren't walking the walk so to speak by storing food, water, doing training now when something bad *isn't* going on -- why would you expect them to suddenly shift gears and do it when something bad *is* going on? More than a little late at that point. Is this person the kind you want to trust the safety of your family to? Not me, thanks...

Being able to earn the trust of someone else and at the same time learn to trust that same someone is no easy task but well worth the effort. The big change for my way of thinking in regards to preparedness came after my wife and I had joined an online preparedness forum. When we joined we really felt that we were in good shape, we had at least six weeks of food on-hand, some water stored, a better than average first aid kit and some weapons – so cool we felt we were good to go.

We were soooo wrong...once we got in and really started reading the articles and personal experience stories from the other members we realized, much to our surprise and dismay, that we had overlooked a large number of things. These included having additional ways to cook the food we had stored, radiation detection and protection, alternative power, chemical protection but most importantly being networked. We had been planning, rather foolishly I might add, to try and go it on our own if there was a problem. I mean I had been in the Marines as well as in law enforcement, was a decent shade tree mechanic – she was a CNA, had been a veterinary technician and knew a good deal about gardening and such so what help did we need?

Turns out quite a bit. For instance, if I was on security and she was working in the garden then who was sleeping? If I was sleeping during the day while she was on security then who was going to fix meals, work on the garden, barter for goods…etc…It was a huge slap in my face when I realized how badly we had not properly planned this out. By being networked with other like minded folks, then there would be manpower for all these things without sacrificing security. It forced a major realignment in our long term plans let me tell you!

Where we were living before we joined the forum was several hours drive on the wrong side of a large mountain range that was routinely closed several times each winter due to weather. We had no other help anywhere close to us that we could depend on. The decision on where to move when the time was right was in no small way influenced by how close some of these same individuals and their families lived.

So what does this mean to you? That depends. If you are determined to try and go it alone, good luck. I am not saying it can't be done -- it can, but the cost in effort, lost sleep and peace of mind to me isn't worth the trade. Networking isn't perfect but nothing is.

Remember to take your time and while doing your search bear in mind that there is likely folks out there that are looking for good, dependable people as well.

-o-

NOTES

14 FUELS

In order to be able to keep your vehicle, your generator, (you do have a generator right?) BBQ, camping stove, etc going you will need to provide them with fuel. Okay so it sounds overly simplistic and even a little obvious but I assure you it is neither. Without fuels our options become very limited in what we will be able to do which includes cooking and heating. Both are very essential to our long term well being.

What type of fuels are we talking about here?

Gasoline	Diesel	Kerosene
Propane	Charcoal	Wood
Wood pellets	Heating oil	Coal

Are you surprised at the number of choices? You may have been, which is totally understandable. We have long been accustomed to simply having to walk over to the thermostat and changing it to either increase the heat or cool us. You need to reassess your thinking in regards to what we have a tendency to take for granted.

Storage Issues

My background in the Fire Service gave me an expanded look into how people and businesses both use and store flammable liquids along with other fuels. The majority of people do a proper job with this. However, too often in this country a tragic fire or explosion occurs due to improper handling and storage of these fuels.

Throughout the book I have talked about the need to add to your prep supplies, the more on-hand the better your options. Fuel is no exception but and I want to stress this point, improper storage in this area is not an option, I cannot stress that strongly enough. If you do this one wrong it could have catastrophic results. Safety is crucial here.

Fuel of some type, be it gasoline for your vehicles, kerosene for your heater, propane for your camp stove is a good thing to have additional supplies of on-hand. This is a no-brainer, however, it doesn't mean that it is something that everyone can do based on where they are living such as an apartment or the amount of space they have in their home such as a condominium.

How can you extend the storage life of your gasoline and diesel? There are several good quality fuel additives commercially available from a variety of retail sources. The best of these are PRI-G and Stabil, both will work with either gasoline and diesel. Kerosene does not need to be treated since it is much less refined that gasoline. It can be treated if you so desire. How long will properly treated stored fuels last?

Gasoline –2 years

Diesel – 4 years

Kerosene – 10 years

The more highly refine a petroleum product is the shorter the storage life. That is critical to understand. Even properly treated gasoline will only store for a few years. Other factors that play a role in storage life are heat and moisture. Both of those work to break down the effectiveness of the fuel. I have personally used fuel (gasoline) that had been treated and stored in excess of six months with no problems whatsoever. That fuel was stored in a garage through a winter in Idaho and was used in the spring.

Storage Safety

As was mentioned above safe storage is incredibly important. The very nature of what we are discussing makes the assorted fuels a fire hazard and even a potential explosive concern. Here are a few tips on safe fuel storage:

Never store fuels near open flames or other heat sources such as water heaters. Liquid fuels can produce vapors and depending upon the ambient conditions those vapors can travel reaching an ignition source if one is nearby. Keep liquids fuels as far as is practical from heat sources.

Keep the fuels in a dry, temperature stable area.

Keep the fuels secure so that children are not able to gain access to them. The potential for poisoning is quite real. Remember that if a child does swallow some liquid fuel do NOT induce vomiting. It is likely that they suffered chemical burns to the throat so vomiting would produce more burns. Contact 911 and the nearest Poison Control center as soon as possible.

Be smart and be safe.

-o-

15 COMMUNICATIONS

In our daily lives we communicate in a variety ways using both verbal and non-verbal means. Our body language, speech patterns, inflections, choice of words, and even the way we dress, can convey the way we are feeling, the mood we are in and much more. We talk to, text, fax and e-mail each other all over the world. Communication is

something that we simply cannot do without. It is so a part of our nature, that we do it without conscious effort or any thought to how we would do it if the current means were no longer available.

The need to communicate is no different when an event occurs. In fact, I would make the argument that it becomes even more important. The ability to give and receive information can mean the difference between making it through a crisis and not surviving. In a crisis, accurate information about what is happening can provide options for your plans, avoid confusion, and help you to resist rumors.... as well as keeping you up-to-date on events. A modest weather radio can keep you ahead of dangerous weather systems. Even the simplest portable radio – battery powered, or "wind-up" self-powered ones -- fill this requirement.

Shortwave Radio is an option for receiving information from outside your region. There has always seemed to be some mystery regarding shortwave radio, but it can be an excellent resource for obtaining information from distant locations. Shortwave radios have multiple "bands", or signal zones – you can receive music, news, sports, and entertain-ment from anywhere in the world, each on different bands.

Generally, the signals are better at night for many foreign stations, simply because of the way the signals pass through the atmosphere. It's fascinating to hear another country's "take" on an event going on around you – the British BBC reports of Katrina were quite different than the ones we heard on regional media. This helps to provide a wider perspective on events, too. Shortwave radios can be found at box stores, at technical stores like Radio Shack, and even online. Name brands will be more pricy and may have features that the lower priced radios don't have. Prices start about $40 and go up to hundreds. For more information on shortwave radio visit www.wavecatcher.us.

Communicating with friends and relatives, though, often becomes vitally important after a calamity. In a crisis, the natural fear for the safety of loved ones can be nearly overwhelming. Just hearing a spouse's or a child's voice will reassure you – and calm them. Don't count on cell phone service to be active in an emergency – during and after the Joplin tornado in 2011, cell transmission towers were damaged and phone service stopped for days to weeks (depending on provider). Landline telephones often will work in a grid-down situation because phone lines are independent of the regular electrical grid – but only if you have a DIRECTLY patched-in phone. That is, not a portable phone; it must be plugged into the physical line.

Instead of cell or landline phone service, private 2-way radios can provide communication when one party goes outside a residence, out to the barn, into the woods, on a hike, or even on a perimeter patrol – keeping everyone connected and alert to any changes in the environment. They can cover an area that may extend a half mile to about 4 miles, depending on the type of hand-held it is. These are some options:

Amateur Radio (HAM) – The growth of amateur

radio in this country has been terrific. HAM provides its user with a wide range of communication options. There are several levels of certification that must be obtained. Basic certification is achieved by passing a test (sample tests are available online). HAM radio operators routinely assist in disaster response, search and rescue operations and much more all around the world on a daily basis. There are both mobile and fixed radio units available. Signals can be sent hundreds or thousands of miles, depending on your set up, antenna, and meteorological conditions. Starter sets begin around $600 and go up from there. For more information on HAM radio visit www.arrl.com or www.qrz.com.

FRS / GMRS Radios – These are small, hand held radios that some refer to as walkie-talkies. The average unit has between twelve and twenty two different channels on it. These can be purchased from a wide array of retail locations all over the country. One drawback to these is that the frequencies used are fixed so that even with different brands and such it is possible to listen in on radio traffic between other people so they are not the best to use for secure communications. They are very cost effective with a pair of radios and a charging unit starting at low as $25 with better quality sets costing upwards of $80 for one set.

Citizens Band Radios – Made popular in the 1970's, CB radio is still a viable method of communicating over long distance. It requires no license to operate and is very cost effective. At peak power, these can transmit signals over 4 miles (depending on terrain). Good CBs can be found at Radio Shack and similar stores, as well as online via ebay.com. Prices for a used battery-powered handheld start around $40; new ones are $99 to $129. You can also acquire models that are mobile and can be mounted in your vehicle for about $130 to $180.

Ideally, one or two types of radios could be on-hand at home, in your vehicles, and available to primary family members – so you can be in touch at a moment's notice if needed. You may wish to store the batteries in a baggie taped to the radio; today's batteries seem to leak more easily than they used to.

-o-

NOTES

16 TOOLS

When, at the urging of a good friend of mine I sat down to start writing this book I wrote out a rough draft of topics and ideas that would be useful. As soon as I wrote down Tools I knew that this was going to be a chapter that I would enjoy putting together.

It was my father who first taught me about tools as I was growing up. The names of the tools, their uses, how to properly care for them, and what not to do so I could avoid injury, were all part of the lessons he taught me. I spent eight years in the military repairing fixed wing jet aircraft and helicopters. After my time in service was over I spent several years working in the emergency services field so the use of tools of all kinds has been a big part of my ability to earn a living.

Tools make the difference between surviving and not

surviving. You want to be able to grow food to keep surviving? Well a shovel, rake and hoe would sure help the process of gardening along and what are they? Tools. Vehicle repairs, plumbing fixes, broken appliances and more all need the application of tools to repair the problems, as well as speed the work. Some jobs are simply not possible without tools. Tim Allen, the great comedian in one of his stand up routines talks about tools, "I don't know what it does but it looks good on my pegboard." While humorous it doesn't convey the seriousness of the issue.

So what kind of tools should a person have? Here is a list I compiled. With these tools, a competent fix-it person could do the majority of repairs a home or vehicle might need. As with most of the lists in this book feel free to add to it or take from it what you want. I have broken the listing down into two sections, hand operated and electrical mixed with other large shop tools.

Hand Tools

Allen wrenches	Assorted "C"clamps
Axe (hand)	Chalk line
Channel lock pliers	Chipping Hammer
Coping saw	Crow's feet sockets
Diagonal cut pliers	File set-regular/jewelers
Hammers (claw/ball peen/roofing/sledge/mallet/deadfall)	Hacksaw
Hand drill	Hand saw

Hoe	Inspections mirror
Mechanical fingers	Needle nose pliers (regular/angled)
Nut runners	Pick
Post hole diggers	Pry bars (assorted sizes)
Punch and chisel set	Rake (leaf/garden)
Rasps	Screwdrivers (flat head/Philips/jeweler sets)
Shovels (irrigation/feed)	Snap ring pliers with attachment
Socket set (¼- 3/8 and ½" drives with extensions)	Stapler
Tap and die set	Telescoping magnet
Torque wrenches (foot/inch pounds)	Vise grip pliers (assorted sizes)
Wire brushes	Wire strippers
Wrench set (standard/metric/box end/offset/line/ratchet/offset ratchet)	

Power Tools / Shop Equipment

Air compressor	Cement mixer
Drill with bits	Drill press
Flammables storage locker	Grinder

Impact wrench and tools	Hand truck
Hydraulic press	Jig saw
Lathe	Light units (500 watt) portable
Miter saw	Oxy/Acetylene torch
Part bins	Parts washer
Sander	Soldering gun with flux and solder
Storage shelves	Table saw
Tarps	Timing light
Tool box	Welder
Wheelbarrow	Work benches

Consumables

Electrical tape	Teflon tape
Solder	Flux
Acid brushes	Electrical wire (all sizes)
Electrical connectors (assorted)	Screws (assorted)
Nuts (assorted)	Bolts (assorted)

Washers (assorted)	Cotter pins (assorted)
Springs (assorted)	O-rings (assorted)
Roll pins (assorted)	WD-40
3 in 1 oil	Grease (assorted weights) tube/can
Rags	Pipe joint compound
Wire (metal) assorted	Cable ties (assorted)
Tooth brushes	Hand cleaner
Welding rods	Parts cleaner
Nails (assorted)	Chalk stick/powdered
String	Rope (assorted)
PVC (pipes/connectors/joints/caps)	Cement
PVC cement	PVC cleaner
Cutting torch gases	Sandpaper (all grits)
Staples	Saw blades (coping/hacksaw/jig)

Assorted hardware, hinges, hooks, hasps, turnbuckles.
Electrical boxes, conduit, fixtures, switches, outlets.
Plumbing, washers, o-rings, valves, pipe, repack kits, tubing,
faucets, spigots.

-o-

So why would we want all of these? First and most important, I am not saying that you *need* all of the items I listed in the three sections above. However, there may be something on there you didn't think of and when you saw it you went, *oh yeah, need one of those.*

Another fact to consider is that the three lists above are in no way complete, there are a number of items that could easily be added to all three. The biggest thing missing is specialty type tools such as brake pliers or hydraulic line wrenches. The lists are there to give you an idea of what is available and useful. Believe me I wish I had all of the tools listed above! The reason for the length of the list is to try and be as thorough as possible.

One of the goals of preparedness is self-sufficiency. In order to get as close as possible to that goal, tools of all sizes and types play a role. Need to fix a pair of eyeglasses? An eight pound sledgehammer, while useful, isn't going to be much help in keeping your glasses on your face. It is a balance between needs, skill, storage space, and financial resources.

So how do you get the tools you need? A few thoughts to help you with this… It is important to buy **quality** tools, brands like Craftsman, Snap-On, S & K, Husky and MAC are among the best. Does this mean it is going to cost you a fortune to outfit a decent tool box? No, start out with a decent tool kit. You can pick these up at Sears, Wal-Mart, Home Depot and many, many places. A good starter tool kit should contain at the least a selection of sockets and the ratchet attachments, several screwdrivers, three or four different styles of pliers, along with a hammer and several wrenches.

To add to this you can look in some other locations to help keep cost down. Garage sales are a great place to pick up tools. Another place to shop is second hand or consignment stores. I had the opportunity a few years ago to pick up a table saw, free standing drill press, and large bench sander for about $200 total. I didn't, which was a mistake. The three machines were older models but still much better than the ones I owned at the time... which was none! Any one of the three units by themselves was worth more than the asking price for all three. When I went back to buy them a few days later they were gone, of course, because someone smartly recognized the bargain that I didn't and pounced on them like I should have. Lesson learned: *strike when the opportunity presents itself.*

Another place I use regularly to add to my tools is the local pawn shops. A number of name brand tools have followed me home from trips to these shops. People will sell off some really nice things in order to raise needed cash. Many times you can pick up quality tools of all types for literally pennies on the dollar. Name brand wrenches that when new are as much as $15.00 I have picked up for under $4.00! It is the same wrench, same brand, might be a little dirty or rusty (but that I can fix) and for a whole lot less than full price!

One other place to look is the local Nifty Nickel publications or Craig's List online which are available in a wide variety of locations. People are often looking to unload quality items for very reasonable sums, and this resource doesn't apply to just tools.

A few notes on tools that are important to bear in mind:

Always *use proper safety equipment* when necessary, gloves, goggles, face shields, etc.

Always *buy quality tools*, they are safer, last longer and are much less likely to fail on you when you really need them.

Clean *your tools* when finished with them and keep them properly stored.

Another factor to consider when mulling the need to purchase tools is that in the case of some type of disaster event, the ability to construct and/or repair could be of huge value in a barter exchange. Say your neighbor has a generator that needs a little work but no tools, in exchange for use of your tools he gives you access to his generator power for a few hours. Be worth something to you? What if someone came to you and they had some broken water pipes that are threatening to flood their basement? Be nice to be able to fix that for them. Turns out they raise chickens, now you have some fresh eggs or fresh food to eat. A barter system will come into being pretty quick following an event. It almost always does. This is, of course, above and beyond the uses you have for the tools for yourself and your situation.

Tools can be the difference between surviving and dying. Take the time to invest in the purchase of quality tools. It won't be a failed investment.

-o-

NOTES

17 BARTER

Our friend Webster's Dictionary defines barter as "To trade goods or services without the use of money." Seems simple enough. So what does this have to do with preparedness? In my opinion, a great deal. You could spend five years and tens of thousands of dollars preparing and there will still be items or information that you could find that you are lacking. This is where having goods and information of your own to offer in trade comes into play.

If you think about it you often use barter now to obtain goods or services already. You might give someone a ride in exchange for them watching the kids later on in the week or watch a neighbor's home while they are away knowing that they will do the same for you next month.

Maybe you are wondering what type of items might be useful for barter? Take a good look around you. What do you use on a regular basis that may be of use to someone else? A great deal, I assure you. This list is by no means even attempting to be complete but to give you an idea of what type of items to be thinking about.

Toilet repair kit	Shoelaces	Matches
Toothpaste	Lighter fluid	Cold medicines
Batteries	Candles	Manual can opener
Soap	Toilet paper	Vegetable seeds
Tools	Light bulbs	Clothes pins
Gasoline	Kerosene	Propane
Spices	Honey	Tea
Cooking oil	Flour	Sugar
Trash bags	Baby formula	Pet food
Water	Liquor	Ammunition

Obviously there are many, many more things that could go on a list of goods such as this so just use your imagination and don't limit yourself. Don't forget that information is a commodity that could be traded as well -- medical training, small engine repair, carpentry and much, much more.

In regards to the last two items I put on the list, liquor and ammunition, a few words of caution. Whether or not to trade these two items away in exchange for what you may need is a personal choice but in my opinion not a good one.

Of the two, my biggest concern by far is ammunition. Why would you trade away something that might be coming at you at some point? Having said that, why put those two items on the list? I am trying to be comprehensive in the information I am giving you. I spoke to a number of my like minded friends and associates regarding these two items and their opinions were split. Most said that it was an individual choice based on the situation. The choice is obviously yours regarding what to trade away or to take in trade but I felt it was important to pass along a warning.

Barter Security

There can be risks when bartering so I wanted to include a few suggestions on how to better protect yourself before, during and after these transactions. The single biggest factor, being safe, is common sense. *If something doesn't seem right, trust that feeling.* Not following our instincts is a failing that happens to all of us. As adults we rationalize it by telling ourselves we are just being silly, or we worry about what someone might say about us, or that we are overreacting. Not true. We have those feelings for a reason. Learn to trust yourself. Better that than getting ambushed because your own pride led you down a path you weren't comfortable with.

Number One Rule - Don't barter at your primary residence whenever possible. This could lead to a situation to where those being traded with decide that since you have some things they could use why not see what else you have. They return later with a larger number of armed friends and try to take all that you have. By "all" I am not just talking about soap and matches either. "All" includes your wife, your daughter, any and everything else that they take a fancy to. There are some seriously evil people out that and they won't hesitate to try and take what's yours. I'm not saying these things to just say them and fill up some space on the page. If you are one of those not accustomed to thinking of people as bad then at some point you need to, and how to deal with them. Your only other option is to give up now.

If you must barter at your home, do all you can to limit what those you are trading with see, and in what quantities. It's none of their business what you have, none at all. Following an event there is confusion, distrust and fear among many other emotions. Having the ability to retain a measure of composure and logical thinking may be the very thing that keeps you and your family/group safe.

Rule Two – Don't try to make a fortune bartering. Keep your "price" reasonable and don't try to get over on someone else. This is important for several reasons. At some point you may be the one in a bad way, and people will remember how you treated them. The moral and legal issues can come back to haunt you in a major way later on, as well. It is vital to remember that there will be social order of some type following an event. Earning a reputation as an unfair trading partner could be a stigma that is hard to erase.

Rule Three – Do NOT talk about how much you have. This is discussed several times throughout the book and I am going to do it here again. I am consciously bringing this up just about everywhere I can get away with it for a reason. News travels in a variety of ways. Just because you didn't think anyone else heard you talking to someone about what you have doesn't mean it didn't happen. Then, there is the person you are trading with. What is to keep them from telling someone else what they were told by you? Not much! So think about not only what you are saying, but who is around to hear it.

Rule Four – Take a different route going to and returning from your bartering. This way if someone is trying to follow you it makes it a good deal harder for them to figure out where you live. This rule may seem like overkill, "Oh, he is being paranoid!" Maybe I am, but a little paranoia may be what keeps you alive. Seriously consider being armed or at least have someone with you that is armed. Sorry if this seems overly cautious or even paranoid -- we are talking about you staying alive and uninjured. You can't do yourself or your family any good if you are dead.

It may be that someone, it could even be you, has the location, security, and amount of goods to coordinate establishing a barter market. I would suggest using the rules above as a guideline to judge the safety of bartering. Someone a long time ago came up with the phrase, "Needs must when the Devil drives." Following an event, especially if it is a large scale situation, the need for certain goods or information could be critically important. Use your common sense and try not to let circumstance overwhelm you.

NOTES

18 WEAPONS

Allow me to start this chapter out by sharing some background on me. Yes, I am a gun owner, in fact I own several. I have owned firearms for nearly all my adult life. I was first given formal firearms training when I went into the Marine Corps, lo these many years ago. I have attended several professional firearms classes since then as well. I shoot IDPA pistol matches when I can. The reason I wanted to share this fact with you is so that you know where I stand on this issue. I am also freely acknowledging that mine is but one opinion of many on the issue.

Firearms are a subject that for some is touchy, to put it mildly. There are those that believe with all their being that the Second Amendment of the Bill of Rights is their Holy Grail. On the other hand, many people in this country, and a host of other nations, do not believe in the private ownership of firearms, period. That debate is NOT one we are going to dwell on here. Suffice to say that if you are not comfortable with the ownership and handling of guns that is entirely your right -- but a point to bear in mind is that it doesn't mean the *other* guy, the one who is forcing his way into your house, is uncomfortable with guns...just a thought.

The purchase of firearms by individuals seeking to add to their means of self protection has increased in recent times due in no small part to the televised pictures from events like the L.A riots and hurricane Katrina, not to mention the uncertainty of the economy. Many, many crimes are stopped or prevented each year due to presence of firearms held by those with the conviction to use them if necessary. Does this mean that merely "waving" a gun of some kind will magically protect you? Of course not. It can even lead to a worse situation.

For this to work firearm ownership **MUST** be coupled with the RESPONSIBLE and SAFE handling and storage of the weapon and its ammunition. There is **NO** excuse or justification out there that allows for the death or injury to someone else, especially a child, due to the negligence of a gun owner.

Owning a firearm is a serious matter and must be approached that way, always. It is important to remember that a gun is a tool, a mechanical device. Like with any mechanical device the potential for misuse if present, a screwdriver could kill someone if used as a weapon. Some states have enacted laws that will charge the parent(s) with a felony if a child is harmed due to negligence involving a firearm. Check your local and/or state regulations for more information on this.

For those who are thinking of acquiring a firearm for protection here are a few things to consider.

- *How comfortable are you with firearms?*
- *How confident are you that you could use the gun against another person if necessary?*
- *Do you have a secure place to keep the weapon(s)?*
- *What is your level of training in handling, firing and maintaining guns?*
- *Are there children in the home?*
- *What kind of weapon do you need?*
- *What are the local, and/or state laws regarding firearm ownership?*

These are but a few of the questions that need answers. The debate over the use of lethal force, for countering an intrusion into a place of residence comes up whether a firearm or any other means of resistance is used. Gun owners MUST be aware of the legal, financial and moral considerations that go hand in hand with owning a firearm.

Firearm Facts

A few basic facts about firearms to help you better understand what we are talking about. Firearms are broken down into three basic categories, handguns, rifles and shotguns. Each of these three types can be further broken down into a VERY large number of sub-categories but we are not going to do that here. Let's take a look at each of the three main categories.

Handguns

This category gets its name from exactly what it implies; these are guns that can be handled usually by just one hand. (*An important safety tip*, whenever possible use **two** hands for better control.) Handguns are also known as pistols.

Pistols are divided into two different but distinct types, the revolver and the semi-automatic. The major differences between the two are how the ammunition is held and how the pistol operates. The revolver uses what is known as a cylinder to hold the ammunition while in the semi-automatics the ammunition is contained in a magazine often within the handgrip to hold and then feed the loaded shells up to be fired.

Semi-auto Walther P22 pistol on the left, Smith & Wesson .357 magnum revolver on the right

The revolver gets its name from the mechanical action of the cylinder. As the trigger is pulled and/or the hammer is moved to the rear manually, the cylinder rotates. This brings the ammunition to a position from which it can be fired. The ammunition capacity of a revolver can be from two to nine cartridges with six being the average.

To fire the semi-automatic pistol, it begins action with one round in the chamber. The shooter pulls the trigger, causing the firing pin to engage. As the firing pin strikes the primer it ignites the powder in the cartridge, forcing the bullet down the barrel under tremendous gas pressure. This gas pressure is essential to the operation of the pistol. Gas pressure forces the upper part of the pistol, known as the slide to the rear. A strong spring then returns the slide forward. The empty shell casing is pulled from the chamber and ejected from the pistol as the slide travels to the rear. As the slide moves forward it strips a fresh cartridge from the top of the magazine and pushes it forward into the chamber. The process can then be repeated until the magazine is empty or the shooter stops pulling the trigger.

It is important to point out at this time that a separate pull of the trigger is required to fire the pistol. Fully automatic weapons, ones in which the gun fires until either the trigger is released or the ammunition is used up, require a special permit from the federal government -- which can be both expensive and difficult to obtain.

.45 Caliber Semi-automatic pistol

Rifles

These are larger than pistols and require the use of both hands to ensure safe and accurate use. Rifles come in bolt action, semi-automatic, and fully automatic versions. A bolt action rifle, often used for hunting, is similar to the action of a revolver in that in order to put a fresh cartridge in position to be fired the shooter must complete a manual operation. In the case of the rifle it is opening the bolt which extracts the shell and replaces it from the magazine as the bolt is moved back forward.

Semi-automatic rifles operate on the same gas pressure principle as semi-automatic pistols. The same can be said for fully automatic rifles. Throughout the history of firearms it has been the rifle that has served as the primary military weapon of the infantry and of the hunter trying to bring meat to the table.

AR-15 Semi-automatic Rifle

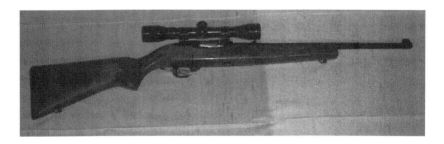

Ruger 10/22 Semi–automatic Rifle

Shotguns

These are firearms similar in size, shape and handling to rifles. The biggest differences between the two are the size of the opening in the barrel and the size/style of ammunition. Typically shotguns are used as hunting weapons and they are especially effective for fowl. The majority of shotguns sold today are what are known as pump action. A slide, positioned underneath the barrel is manually pulled to the rear clearing the spent casing from the weapon and moving a loaded one into position. There are quality semi-automatic shotguns available on the market as well.

12 Gauge Pump Action Shotgun with modified stock (one piece with pistol grip)

Ammunition

The proper term for a complete unit, or round, of ammunition is a cartridge. A complete cartridge consists of several components all of which are essential to the unit. These components are:

Bullet – This is the part that leaves the barrel of the weapon and strikes the target. The one difference with this is shotgun rounds which contains pellets.

Powder – The propellant used to create the gas pressure that forces the bullet out of the weapon.

Primer – A small charge that when activated ignites the powder.

Casing – This is the metal tube, closed off at one end that holds the powder, primer and the bullet.

To identify ammunition look on the bottom, *most* ammunition is stamped with the abbreviation of the manufacturer and the caliber. The usual exception to this rule is .22 caliber and that is due to the small size of the casing. It may say something similar to *WIN 9mm Luger* which means it is a cartridge manufactured by the Winchester company and is a standard 9 millimeter round.

Safe Firearm Handling Guidelines

There is an old saying among hunters and other shooters that there are two types of shooters: those who have had an accident and those who will. I don't know if I agree with that. Having been around firearms for much of my life, and having had several opportunities to undergo formal firearms training both military and civilian, I can admit to having two accidental discharges. But because I had not lapsed on all the safety rules of firearms handling I can happily report that no injuries occurred as a results of my mistakes (other than the ones to my own ego). In this section I do something I very rarely do, which is to use absolutes such as always and never. Gun safety is one of those rare times when I feel that absolutes are essentials.

- ✓ *Never handle firearms or any other type of equipment if you are under the influence of drugs or alcohol.*
- ✓ *Always handle each weapon as if it loaded even if you suspect it isn't*
- ✓ *Always keep the weapon pointed in a safe direction such as toward the ground.*
- ✓ *Always keep your finger off the trigger until you are ready to shoot.*
- ✓ *Be certain of your target and what is beyond it.*
- ✓ *Never have unsecured firearms where children can reach them.*
- ✓ *Always safely store and secure your firearm.*

✓ *Before handling a firearm have an understanding of how it works.*

✓ *Use proper ear and eye protection when shooting.*

✓ *Do not believe everything that you see on the Internet. You need to check out the facts for yourself.*

I know that some, if not most of these rules, especially the first one, seem so basic that they don't need to be said. Every one of these rules exists because at some point, someone (or numerous some ones over the years) didn't follow the proper procedure. Firearm safety is too important to take glibly.

I have some friends who suffered the most horrific loss any parent can, the death of a child. They were visiting some friends and staying overnight. During the night their young child got up and found an unsecured weapon and was able to fire it. The child died from his injuries. Years later they are still trying to come to grips with the event. There are no words, no actions, no comfort that can bridge that gap. It is much too important for apathy.

Firearms Training

The subject of training appears throughout this book for a reason. Having acquired certain skills in order to be better prepared these same skills will not serve you unless you practice and stay sharp with them. Firearms are no different and are one skill that *will* deteriorate without practice. The ability to accurately place a bullet on the proper spot the first time is no gimmick or magic trick. Those individual who make their living as professional competitive shooters may fire as many as 100,000 rounds a year between training and competitions. I am not suggesting that you need to approach that level but it reinforces the point that training is essential.

So where is this training available? In many parts of the country firearms training is available in a surprisingly large number of venues. Gun stores with firing ranges offer firearms training in many instances, some Police Departments offer periodic training, sport shooting clubs such as those for trap and skeet, will sometimes offer this training as well.

Another resource to check is the National Rifle Association which can be found online at www.nra.org. The N.R.A. has taught millions of people in this country of all ages, backgrounds and abilities to safely handle and shoot firearms. They offer courses in numerous locations throughout the country all year for pistols, rifles and shotguns. Their prices are reasonable and the training is certified.

The Survival Battery

There are those among the survival minded that feel that firearms are the answer to all preparedness situations. They arm themselves with the notion that more and bigger is better. They spend thousands of dollars on fancy, high tech rifles with incredible long range optics, dozens upon dozens of magazines and untold amounts of ammunition but then they stop. They don't buy food in large quantities, store fuel and water, stockpile medical supplies or maybe worst of all, don't network with other like minded individuals. Their whole attitude toward survival is a firearm-based movie illusion of street fighting and battling off hordes of ravaging, starving people – in which they are the hero who triumphs without mussing his hair.

It is stupid, short sighted and will not work, period. If someone tells you different, do yourself a favor, thank them politely and then as soon as you possibly can, excuse yourself and get the hell away from them. They are idiots, and scariest thing is that they are well armed idiots.

Firearms are NOT, repeat NOT, the be-all and end-all of preparedness. Do firearms have a role in preparedness? Yes, I genuinely believe that they do. But it is not a primary role. Firearms are a tool. They have their role and function within the context of survival the same as a screwdriver or spare set of lantern mantles. If you have to resort to actually defending your family by firing on someone, then things are really, really bad. There is a lot more to preparedness and living well under trying circumstances, before any kind of shooting starts.

For example, following hurricane Katrina there were many neighborhoods all over the Gulf Coast region where the residents banded together and formed armed watch groups to protect themselves and their property from becoming victims of crime. This action saved a number of homes from being looted. During the Rodney King riots in Los Angeles in the 1990's many shop owners were able to keep their businesses protected from the mobs at times merely by displaying the firearms they had. Firearms can be an effective tool to deter crime.

So what is the "survival battery"? It is a group of

several firearms that cover nearly all the basic situations that a firearm might be called on to be used in.

In my opinion the minimum firearms you should own are:

---**A quality pistol** in one of the following calibers, 9 millimeter, .45 ACP, .357 magnum or .40 Smith & Wesson. Believe me when I say that that I know this statement will cause a ton of disagreement among the firearm conscious readers. What about this caliber, or why did he pick those…These recommendations are based on my experience and opinion. Does it mean that these are the only choices you should consider? No. It is a matter of personal choice but these four calibers are among the most effective in proven stopping power based on actual shooting incidents.

---**A quality semi-automatic .22 caliber rifle**. A good example of this is the Ruger 10/22 rifle. It is compact, accurate, easy to shoot, a breeze to clean and best of all, reasonably priced. This is one of the most popular semi automatic rifles ever made and a must have weapon for many shooters. Countless numbers of shooters have been trained to shoot using this quality, accurate weapon.

---**A quality rifle**. Notice I didn't say "a machine gun," or an "assault rifle." A rifle that is well made, accurate, clean, loaded and *in hand* is worth more than the gee whiz *wundergun* that you have been eyeing at the local gun shop. A buddy of mine has a really nice lever action 30-30' carbine that he loves. He shoots it as often as he can and is pretty good with it. He doesn't want anything else so for him it works fine. Does it mean that if you have, for instance, an

AR style rifle that it won't work? Of course it will but so will an 1898 Mauser or a Ruger Mini-14, both of which are much less expensive than one of the AR style rifles.

---**A quality shotgun** will complete the quartet. Preferably purchase either a Mossberg or Remington. The Mossberg Model 500 is accurate, reliable, and reasonably priced. With the Remington, a Model 870 is an excellent choice. Both weapons have been around for years and have proven themselves over and over. There are an astounding number of quality after-market accessories that you can pick up for these weapons that enhance their operation and usefulness. Both are accurate, easy to maintain with a cornucopia of ammunition choices. I have owned examples of both.

That's it; those four weapons will provide you with a variety of means to handle nearly any shooting situation. If you notice there is one word that appeared in all four categories. The word is *quality*. Spend the money to get a quality firearm. Something to consider in this vein is that something that is expensive doesn't mean it is quality, and by the same token if something is inexpensive doesn't make it a piece of junk. Stick with the name brands and don't be afraid to ask questions, lots of questions. If you going to make an investment in something that could save your life, isn't it worth doing some research on it? I absolutely think so.

In addition, shooting is a fun sport. Target shooting is something I deeply enjoy. The ability to, with skill, place a bullet two hundred and fifty yards away on the exact spot that you want, is something that can't be beat. It is the same kind of feeling a golfer gets when they get that great swing just right and the ball flies far and straight right down the fairway. One of the beauties of shooting is that shooting for fun, like golf or virtually any other sport, is also training. The more you do something, the better you get at it.

What To Buy In What Order?

I was recently asked this question and honestly it took me a moment to think about it. Not because I didn't have an answer but the realization that I had to look at it from the perspective of someone who wasn't coming from a background with firearms. My recommendation is to start with a quality pistol that you are comfortable with. This is where having a shooting range within a reasonable distance really helps. The ability to handle and fire a selection of pistols prior to purchasing the one you are comfortable with is a major plus. Another advantage of buying a pistol is that it is smaller than a rifle or shotgun.

If you choose to apply for a Concealed Weapons Permit (if your local jurisdiction allows that) then you are armed all the while not appearing to be. It is also easier to secure a handgun than it is a rifle or shotgun. Small safes are much less expensive than a full size unit. In addition the safe can be used to house important personal documents, which should be secured as a matter of course, anyway.

A quality pistol will likely cost you less than $600 dollars. I am sure some of you are saying "$600?! That is too much!" Please note I said less than that. A good revolver can be had for under $350. After the pistol I would move on to the .22 rifle then a shotgun and finish up with the rifle. It allows you to slowly expand your battery of firearms while building up your experience and training as you add each new firearm.

It's also important to understand that it is completely fine to be uncomfortable about owing or even just handling firearms. Not everyone is a "gun person." By that I mean owing them, being around them a great deal while growing up, shooting on a regular basis. Firearms can be intimidating to those not familiar with them. So if you are not a "gun person," don't despair or get to feeling intimidated by them. A pistol or rifle is a tool, nothing more, nothing less. YOU control it, not the other way around. When the time is right and you are comfortable with owning a firearm, then you will.

If you or your partner is smaller framed then consider NOT rushing out to fire off a twelve gauge shotgun -- I assure you it is a handful. Start out with smaller calibers and work your way up to the larger ones. If you rush into it then the noise, recoil and such can keep you or them from getting to a comfort level, which won't allow the person to keep at it. Firearm training takes time and effort along with the right mental attitude. Fear isn't always bad. It's good to fear something enough to respect it. But don't let that fear overwhelm you.

This chapter is labeled Weapons. It is important to remember that it isn't just firearms that you can acquire and train with, but also that other weapons can provide defense as well as pose risks to you, too. Don't think a crossbow is much of a problem? Think again, hunters have used crossbows for centuries as hunting weapons. One big thing in their favor is that they are considerably quieter than a rifle. The same can be said of the use of bow and arrows. Modern compound bows are extremely accurate in the hands of someone who knows how to properly use it. Me, personally, I have no desire at all to be the recipient of a razor tipped broad head arrow designed for the taking of large game animals. Talk about leaving a wound!

So the key is to not to get locked into a certain mindset. A screwdriver can be used as a deadly weapon, too, so awareness of what is going on around you is important.

So To Summarize...

If you are on the fence so to speak about buying a firearm, pull out the yellow pages and check under Gun Stores. Many of these have indoor shooting ranges and will often rent weapons for a very reasonable amount which would allow you to try out different weapons in a safe, controlled environment with instructors at hand. They can answer your questions in person. It is in their best interest to give good guidance, because they want your business.

Firearm ownership is a serious responsibility. You MUST approach it that way. Buy quality, then practice safe and responsible storage and handling of all your weapons.

Proficiency is not a once learned and then forgotten skill. In order to maintain your ability to hit what you are aiming at, practice, practice and, oh yeah, more practice. On average, shooting 100 rounds a month per weapon is an *absolute minimum* to establish baseline proficiency. More practice is better.

Buy quality name brand ammunition to cycle through your weapons. Brands like PMC, Remington, Winchester, CCI, and Federal are all quality. If you only have one shot to try to keep you alive, make sure it is a good one.

Keep your weapons clean and buy spare parts for them as you can. Make it one of the things that you do regularly. Even if you don't shoot often you should still clean your weapons on a regular basis. Write it on the calendar, 17th of each month or whatever day you pick, clean your guns. Have a stock of cleaning gear on-hand. I personally recommend the Hoppes No. 9 powder solvent. Great stuff. Cleaning kits and supplies are available in a wide variety of retail outlets and are reasonably priced. Having one of these kits with a stock of supplies is no different from having a can of beans on-hand. Both play a role in being prepared.

Talk to your friends who own firearms. Ask them to let you handle them and ask questions. Remember safety first and always. Ensure that the weapon is unloaded and keep it pointed in a safe direction, meaning away from people, animals and buildings.

Be smart, be safe, and have fun.

-o-

19 HEALTH

Throughout the book I have touched on the importance of staying properly hydrated, ensuring that food preparation is sanitary, personal hygiene is addressed and more. The reason for these guidelines is to help you and yours stay as healthy as possible. This is especially true before an event. Believe me, telling yourself that "Oh, if something happens that will shape me up" you are fooling yourself and letting your family down.

Now -- not then -- is the time to lose those fifteen pounds you keep telling yourself you want to, quit smoking, drink only in moderation and learn to eat right. *Now*, not after the fact. Chances are you may end up having to do all that after an event anyways depending upon what is going on. Better to start now and be used to living the right way.

Do I sound like one of those health nuts you might be

sick of hearing? I'm not trying to, but it is important. Say the area you live in gets hit by severe weather or some other kind of natural disaster. You have damage to the house, trees down, no power, no running water and your family needs to be taken care of, now, right now. They are scared, there's water coming in through the broken windows, shattered glass everywhere. What are you going to do? Ten minutes of exertion and you are sweating up a storm, breathing hard because you have no cardio-vascular endurance and you still have hours and hours of hard work to do. Will you get in shape at that rate? Maybe, but I doubt it. More likely you will injure yourself through over-exertion, pull a muscle or suffer a heat injury or worse, a heart attack. What will your family do then? They depend on you and will need your help especially during this time.

Taking care of yourself is no different than making sure you have a stock of supplies and equipment. You are the most important resource that you have available to you, so making sure you're operating properly is key. Having a diverse menu will aid in keeping your energy levels up both prior to and following an event, as well. If there is the ability to create meals that are hot, flavorful and tasty it will go a long way to making you and your family feel better as well as providing your body with the essential energy it needs. We talked about this in the Food chapter as well so I know that this isn't something new for you to be reading about. You're a smart person, believe that.

Cut down on the fatty, sugary food that tends to dominate many of our meals. Add more fruit and vegetables to your meals. If you are not in the greatest shape make sure that you start out s-l-o-w-l-y. Do not jump into a training regimen like you are training for a triathlon. Begin with brisk walks that get you out of the home, and begin to improve your cardio-vascular endurance. Check with your doctor for tips on better eating and exercise. The key is consistency. Keep at it.

In 2010 I went through a period of not feeling well, numerous painful muscle spasms, lack of energy and so went to the doctor and with a little testing was informed that I am a Type 2 diabetic. I was stunned. I had no idea. The health concerns were directly related to how poorly I was eating and so some major changes took place. Since then I have dropped twenty pounds and eat much smarter. I run three times a week, something I couldn't have done then. I feel a good deal better also. Regular checkups are a very good thing.

DENTAL – Get your teeth taken care of, and keep your dental health maintained. Can you imagine trying to deal with no power and damage to your house all the while having a throbbing tooth ache? Not me, thank you very much. Properly brush and floss your teeth on a regular basis as well as having dental visits. Poor dental health will, without a doubt, be a major problem during a calamity event.

MENTAL – I feel strongly that this area is one that is often overlooked in preparedness. The mental effects of an event on a person can range from almost nothing to catastrophic, depending upon the type and severity of whatever caused the incident. This in turn could lead to a person's stress level being drastically elevated as they attempt to respond to and cope with the situation. Stress is hard on the body and mind. Prolonged stress is not healthy and it can eventually lead to other health issues, some of them quite serious.

Dealing with an elevated stress level can be difficult. Many of the options available to us in non-event times such as outings with friends, a long drive in the car, a few drinks at the bar, a meal out, taking in a movie, or surfing the internet, will likely be completely unavailable following an event. So the stress can build without the usual outlets to lower it. Being aware of the added stress is a big help. Can't fix a problem if you aren't aware of it.

How to properly address the problem during and following an event can be difficult but not impossible. Here are a few examples of what might be useful post-fan to help reduce stress.

A good hot meal – Food has long been a comfort to us. Having a warm, tasty meal can help reduce stress as well as help better regulate bodily functions.

Reading – The ability to "escape" your current reality can be used to help relax you. But, as with all of these suggestions, don't become obsessed with trying to get away from what is going on around you. You need to stay grounded -- but being able to detach for a little while can be helpful.

Sleep – The importance of being well rested cannot be overstated. Will it be easy to get the rest you will need? Maybe not, but it is one of the most effective means of making you feel better. As human beings we function at a higher level when we are rested.

Physical activity – This may seem strange to see on a list of things meant to relax you. I know for me the act of working on something can itself be therapeutic. The satisfaction of taking on a job and working through it until completion is a great feeling.

Intimacy – With this I'm not talking about just the act of intercourse although that is certainly one aspect of it. I am also talking about doing small acts of kindness and selflessness such as giving your spouse/partner a back rub, a kind sincere word they need, and so much more. If there is a major crisis or event then the stress level could be very high and working with someone to get through it seems to make more sense than trying to go it alone. Remember all the reasons that you are with that person. It's important.

So keeping yourself healthy in all aspects physically, mentally and emotionally is challenging enough at times but if you are ever caught up in a crisis situation then you may need to consciously remind yourself to take stock of where you are and how you're feeling. Don't be afraid to admit that you're frustrated, angry, or that the fear of the situation is getting to you. Being able to do that makes you stronger, not weaker.

-o-

NOTES

20 N.B.C.

Looking at the Table of Contents some of you may have wondered what this chapter was going to be about. A completely legitimate question! What we are talking about here are the big three in the world of Weapons of Mass Destruction (WMD) - Nuclear, Biological and Chemical weapons. In some quarters this is also known as CRBN which is Chemical, Radiological, Biological and Nuclear.

Over the course of human evolution man has progressively developed deadlier and deadlier weapons both for food procurement as well as warfare -- from the days of sticks and rocks to swords to bows to the firearms of today. The big three represent the current height of man's ability to kill his fellow man. The risks that these weapons pose is one that must be acknowledged no matter how distasteful.

It is completely understandable to be uncomfortable thinking about the precautions needed to protect you and your family from these weapons. In my opinion this area of planning, training and buying involves a good deal more specialization than any of the others discussed in this book. Part of this is due to the fact that what we are trying to protect ourselves from is something that we can't see. Yes, while a nuclear blast is visible, the radiation it produces isn't -- which is the same with germs and other microscopic enemies. It is our nature to fear what we don't understand and can't see. In this case there is in fact much to fear. Let's take a closer look at each of the three categories.

The history of chemical weapons dates back to ancient times when attackers would use catapults to hurl the dead, diseased carcasses of animals, and sometimes corpses of people, into walled cities they were attacking to spread sickness to weaken the defenders. Numerous regimes over the course of history have used the WMD's available in their time. One of the most widespread uses of chemical weapons was during World War I. Mustard gas (chlorine) and other weapons created large amounts of horrific casualties on both sides. Entire units were sometimes affected.

Some of the most recent examples of the use of WMD would be from Iraq when it was under the control of Saddam Hussein. During the eight year long Iran-Iraq war (1980-1988) the Iraqi's used chemical weapons against their opponent, as well as against different ethnic groups within Iraq itself such as the Kurd's. The use of these weapons inflicted casualties that, according to some reports, number 30,000 dead.

Terrorists have used WMD's also. In 1995 Japan, a cult known as Aum Shinrikyo released Sarin, a deadly nerve agent, on several Tokyo subway trains. This sent over 3,000 people seeking medical care and killed twelve. Nine months prior to the Tokyo attack they also released Sarin in a town west of Tokyo exposing 300 and killing seven.

Here in the United States we have not been immune to the effects of biological terrorism either. In 1984, in the small town of The Dalles, located in north central Oregon, a group of religious followers known as the Rajhneeshees intentionally tainted a number of restaurant salad bars with *Salmonella Typhimurium* in an attempt to sicken enough people to be able to influence a local election in their favor. Over 750 people were sickened by the group. An investigation later proved that members of the group were involved and arrests were made. Several group members served prison sentences for their involvement in the attacks. Fortunately, no one died as a result of their exposure.

A more recent example of this was the anthrax letters sent to the offices of two U.S. Senators and several media outlets in September of 2001. These letters, which contained anthrax spores, killed five people and infected seventeen more. The FBI investigation lasted for years into this case, and in their words was "one of the largest and most complex in the history of law enforcement."

-o-

It is important to have a little better understanding of what these weapons are.

Biological Agent – This is a toxic or infectious agent that may be used against living targets by making them sick or incapacitated – "weaponized" bacteria and viruses.

Nerve Agent – A gas or liquid that affects the body's ability to transmit commands along the nerve network. This results in a body becoming unable to coordinate breathing and circulation, with death or incapacitation as the result.

Nuclear / Atomic arms – The primary injuries are heat and blast damage to the body but radiation is a serious concern.

A number of countries around the world, including the United States, have stockpiles of all of these types of weapons which make them a real threat. The United States is for now the only nation to have used atomic weapons in a time of war. I believe history will one day show that we were the first but not the last to do that.

In regards to nuclear weapons there are a number of myths out there that I would like to take a look at and try to dispel.

Myth – *No one would survive a nuclear war so there is no need to prepare.*

Reality: This fallacy has been around for decades and it simply isn't true at all for a number of reasons:

- The world population is too widely scattered for everyone to be killed.

- A number of countries have elaborate Civil Defense infrastructures in place that would provide protection to a number of people.
- Despite advances in warhead designs over the years some will miss their targets and strike less populated areas

Myth – *All food and water will be contaminated by radioactive fallout.*

Reality: Sealed food containers will not be susceptible to fallout. Water taken from supply locations such as lakes and reservoirs that do receive fallout can be filtered to eliminate the contamination. Fruits and vegetables can be washed and peeled.

Myth – *All buildings and supporting infrastructure will be completely destroyed.*

Reality: In proximity to the blast area structural damage will be the highest. The further you are away from the blast zone the less likely damage will occur. With a ground burst the primary means of damage are caused by heat and overpressure. Certainly there will be damage to buildings, electrical lines, communications equipment and the like but not to the point of total loss.

Myth – *A nuclear blast will ignite everything in the area.*

Reality: Within a certain distance from the blast the heat wave will certainly ignite fires but that damage zone reduces rapidly the further away you are from the blast.

Myth – *A large nuclear exchange involving large number* *of weapon detonations will create a nuclear winter effect, which will kill most people in the hemisphere with arctic cold.*

Reality: This was challenged and disproved in the mid 1980's. Certainly areas around concentrations of detonations will be affected, but the fear of a global debris cloud reducing the sunlight and lowering temperatures enough to cause a winter effect is false.

N.B.C Equipment

What type of equipment is recommended to help detect harmful agents and protect you from them?

Radiation Meters – Once widely available these meters detect radiation and display the levels on a gauge.

Dosimeters – These are devices designed to worn by a person to monitor the amount of radiation exposure that a person is receiving.

Detection Paper – Touching the paper to suspected points of chemical contamination causes the paper to change color depending upon the agent.

Masks – Talking about military style gas masks here, not the paint store dust masks.

Coveralls – The most widely known brand is Tyvek© which are available to the public through a variety of retail sources.

Example of a Victoreen CDV-717 Radiation Meter

Trying to find quality, calibrated radiation meters and dosimeters isn't easy. You can find meters from various online sources including ebay, but finding ones that are properly calibrated is the issue. Since civil defense went out of vogue in this country some time back much of the equipment supply has dried up.

-o-

What Are Some Ways To Avoid Being A Victim?

First and foremost is to not be there. Avoid, as much as is practical, any areas that would make good targets, such as subways and crowded public venues (sports events, concerts, and so on). This may sound as if I am telling you to live in fear and never, ever go out. Nothing could be further from the truth. The best advice on dealing with terrorists

I've ever heard is this: Live your life as you see fit. It drives them crazy.

Exercise caution, be cognizant of any alerts relating to terrorism. Stay informed as to what is going around you. Is there a special event downtown today that the governor and other high officials will all be present for? Possibly a good target for an extremist. Situational awareness plays a huge role in personal safety and this is a very good example of that.

Have a family emergency plan. Teach everyone where to go in case of emergency. Practice your plan on a regular basis since situations do change.

Have a safe area identified in your home. For chemical exposures, this should be on an upper level since many chemical agents are heavier than air. For radiation exposure, the deeper in the earth or more central to the building (with "mass" around it), the better it is. Keep duct tape and plastic sheeting on-hand to seal windows and doors should it prove necessary.

Be prepared to wash and dispose of the liquid away from your immediate location. Skin absorption is one of the primary contamination routes. Washing with warm water and soap, or Dawn dish soap, or a water/bleach solution (10/1 ratio) will help reduce this.

NBC can be a very frightening thing but with some common sense, training and the right supplies it can be much less concerning.   –o–

21 THE TOUGH QUESTIONS

You have already read through a good deal of the information and might be feeling somewhat overwhelmed. Understandable, but too bad. This is the reality of the world and it can be an overwhelming place at times. I honestly don't mean to sound callous but living a preparedness lifestyle means that you do look at the worst case situation. Often that is the first one you look at. You plan for the worst *and hope for the best.* That may sound trite but it really is an accurate way of looking at it.

So are you ready for a look at some of the harder issues that you may be forced to deal with? I hope so, because these issues could be coming to visit you whether you want them to or not. Preparedness in real life is nothing at all like it might be in some books or worse, movies. It's not going to be about running gun battles in the street on a daily basis. If that is the situation you're in, then you're really in deep trouble and its w-a-y past time to go someplace else! No, what I am talking here about are the day-in-day-out issues that you will have to deal with that are not glamorous at all but potentially just as deadly. Starvation, illness, loss of hope…

So how do those things, the daily challenges, become just as deadly as the "big" threats? Let's take a look at starvation for example. You have some food on-hand, a means to cook it, but it's only enough for your family and even with that it will require some stretching to make it last for any length of time. You've been adding to your pantry and other supplies as you can but it takes time to build up a stock. Are you prepared to have your unprepared in-laws, parents, siblings and their families, friends and co-workers or any combination of these people to show up on YOUR doorstep following an event, expecting you to take care of them? You're not? Why not? How far will that food stretch now? This situation has happened to many, many people in the past and it will happen in the future. A one-year supply for two is only six months for four and only three months for eight and so on.

Avoiding this is part of the reason that keeping your mouth shut about being prepared is so vitally important. Why should these other people spend their money to prep? You already have, so why should they? Hey, you're family so you should take care of them! I promise you that this is how some of them will feel about it. And feel strongly, possibly strongly enough to demand the help if it is not forthcoming; even get ugly about it, demanding that you open up your home to them despite that fact they may make more money than you do. Logic and rational thought go away real quickly when people are scared and/or confused. What matters to them at that point is their safety and *only* their safety. If you are the family prepping guru, guess who is going to get an unexpected visit?

So what do you tell these relatives, etc when they make a comment along the lines of "If something happens I know where I'm going!"? Meaning, your house. Have you given that any thought at all? If you haven't I highly suggest that you do. Here are a couple of suggestions for you to consider using if this situation happens to you.

Tell them if they are coming to come supplied - Hand them a copy of the Entry Goods list and tell them that this is the *minimum* that you expect them to bring (copy of the list is in the Entry Goods chapter) and make sure that they understand that YOU ARE NOT KIDDING. Make sure they understand that just showing up with Entry Goods doesn't mean it ends there.

There will be tasks they will be expected to help with also, such as cleaning, child care and discipline, security, meal preparation, gardening and more. Entry Goods are not a get-in and do-nothing license. Entry Goods are only the beginning of their contribution, not the ending. The more they bring or have already pre-positioned the better, provided that they bring the proper supplies and not a carload of just stuff.

"Fine, c'mon over but I won't be home (and I'm taking my stuff with me)." – You tell that your plan is to leave and head for the hills. It may not be true but disinformation can work in your favor. If they think that you won't be home then it might be enough incentive for them to do something for themselves. I am not saying it is a guarantee that they won't come anyway, but it will hopefully make them be more proactive.

Put them to work – If they do show up empty handed then they can barter labor for food, shelter and protection. There will always be plenty of work to do, raising food, standing security, caring for children and more. There will be plenty for everyone to do and it will take the efforts of all those that contribute to get the work taken care of. Now, understand I am **NOT** telling you to create a forced labor camp using family members, neighbors or whoever as the inmates. Not only is both immoral and illegal, it creates a host of problems on its own. A reasonable exchange of labor for food and such is one thing, slavery is another. They must understand that if they don't work, they must leave.

Show up and I'll shoot you – A very strong and serious statement. Some will take it to heart; others will see it as a threat and decide to take you out first. No warning, no apologies. In addition there are the legal and moral issues involved with shooting someone, especially if they are unarmed. (At some point, some degree of order will be established; it may not be what we consider today to be "normal.") There will be some return to normalcy and with it some degree of social law and the consequences of shooting someone could be serious, really serious. Another down side is that they may get to thinking, "If he is willing to shoot me then he must have tons of stuff he's protecting!"

Obviously these are by no means the only options regarding what you can tell people but it hopefully gives you a good starting point. The most important factor to consider is that there is no such thing as a free ride especially when those people coming to you are potentially taking resources away from you and your family which is where your primary responsibility should be.

-o-

So let's talk about illness a bit. Does anyone in your household have special health conditions that require medications: heart condition, diabetes, mental illness? What happens when there are no more medications on-hand and the means to get more is for now not available? Building up a stockpile of medications can be done, it takes time but it is possible. Speak to your doctor and find out about having some additional meds on-hand. If the medication allows a refill and you don't need it right then, get the refill and store it. Put it in a zip lock baggie or vacuum seal and label it for the condition it treated. Discretely ask your pharmacist about any long-term storage problems.

Some medications do become toxic at some point while other medications will slowly lose some potency over time but the way I see it, some potency is better than none at all, so hang on to your older medications. Keep the medication in its original container (you don't really want to be in a situation where your goods might be searched and you have dozens of little baggies with unidentified pills) and at a reasonably constant temperature (meaning don't toss it in a bag in the back of the car for storage!). That should help increase the shelf life.

Illness could also result from a lack of cleanliness, both in personal hygiene and of the items needed to sustain daily life. Food preparation areas and equipment in particular need to be kept clean. Clean as in sanitary not just clean to the eye. Think about how bad a bout of food poisoning is right now when quality medical care is available as are store bought medications. Following an event, if someone comes down with a major case of vomiting and diarrhea, if not properly treated the loss of excessive amounts of fluid could bring on dehydration which can be life threatening. Lack of personal hygiene is just as important and easy to overlook since people will be tired, frustrated and trying to cope with the changes occurring in their world. Eating without washing hands allows for the bacteria and other microscopic organisms to enter the body and lead to sickness.

A big concern with this is that it takes at least one person away from the work that needs to be done and worst case the illness affects the entire group. Children and the elderly are considered at a higher risk due to the fact their immune systems are not as efficient at providing protection. One way to address this is have a supply of cleaning wipes on-hand. The type that come out of the top of the container and are already embedded with cleaning solution. It's not ideal but better than nothing. Don't use the ones with bleach in them for personal use, those are for cleaning areas, not people. Have your people wash their hands several times a day, especially before meals, and keep the general area sanitary, especially the food preparation and storage areas.

One aspect of this to consider is that here in the United States we aren't used to ingesting food and drink of marginal quality which in many countries around the world IS the norm. This means our bodies have less resistance to food and water borne problems.

-o-

A question that no one really wants to have to consider is "What are you going to do if someone in your group dies?" this is not a pleasant thought but we are human and have a finite life span. Factor in illness, lack of medication, or a loss of hope and that time span can be reduced a great deal.

In coming to terms with someone passing there are some additional questions. Are there any special religious or ethnic rituals that will need to be observed? Is there an area that could be used for burial? What about burning the body? Is that acceptable or even practical? Do you have any idea of why the person died? Was it due to illness or heart failure, maybe some type of trauma? All these questions, and more, will have to be addressed and before it happens because you don't want to have to come up with all the answers while trying to deal with the grief and emotional upheaval.

Not saying that you have to have every single detail worked out ahead of time but at it needs to be thought about. Then there is the emotional effort required to deal with the loss - it can cause a loss of focus, anger, depression and more. It can be an emotional roller coaster which will likely not be fun and can seriously threaten a group's survival.

-o-

How will you handle trash disposal? What are you going to do with all the empty food cans, boxes and containers? If there are no trash trucks running how does all the trash get handled? Burning it might not be practical since the smoke and smell could travel a good distance. Burying it is another choice but over time the amount will add up to a sizable quantity. Plus there are those for whom burial is not an option for at all such as apartment dwellers.

We are a society of thoughtless waste. We will need to give serious thought to how we can use and re-use what we now consider to be "waste". There is the most obvious example of composting but you need to know what can and cannot be composted. In addition it takes time for material to decompose sufficiently to make worthwhile compost. Worn or torn clothing can be cut down for smaller adults or children or can be cut and twisted and sewn for rugs or make into quilts. Do you have needles, pins, and thread?

What about vermin control? This is part of the illness discussion we spoke about above. It is important to keep areas as clean as possible, waste collected and disposed of. Failure to do so can lead to an issue in having vermin drawn to your area. Having a supply of rodent traps and poison on-hand is a smart move. Remember you can't control everything around you but you will have some measure of control over what happens in your area so work toward that.

-o-

I am sure that right now it seems like I am the bearer

of nothing but bad news. While I would love to dispute that, I really can't. I am not bringing all this up simply to depress or discourage you. I am just trying to provide you as much information as I possibly can so that you have the ability to make better decisions based on facts not conjecture. I can honestly say that I understand it is a great deal of information to try and process. This is part of the reason that throughout the book I have touched on doing things at a steady pace compared to jumping in and running with it. It takes time to properly prep. That is why it's a lifestyle not a fad or project for the weekend.

You have to get out and take a hard look at your situation. If you are realistically planning on several more people coming to stay with you then where are they going to park their vehicles, sleep, how will meals be prepared and eaten, how about laundry and personal hygiene? Trying to come up with all the answers for these questions and the others that will come up may prove very difficult. Better to give it some thought now when it is easier. The answers you provide now may not prove to be workable when something actually occurs but it gives you a solid starting place. It is very helpful to write down your ideas. It is always easier to go back and review something in writing rather than trying to draw out it from memory when there might be a host of other things going on.

This chapter was titled **The Tough Questions** for a reason. Making sure that you can face up to these questions may not be easy for some readers but I have worked hard to this point to give you a realistic view of preparedness. I don't intend to let you down now.

NOTES

22 SECURITY

I deliberately wanted to save this chapter until the end due to the importance of it. Before going deeper into this I want to share with you some of my back ground in this area so that you have a better understanding of where I am coming from.

I have over twelve years experience in private security and law enforcement. I have worked as a Corrections Officer in a maximum security prison, casino security officer, provided security in a hospital as well as owned my own security consulting firm and more. I was also founder and co-owner of a security guard company serving a number of retail customers. In addition I served as Security/Safety Director for a federal facility. Among the certifications I earned along the way was that of a Personal Protection Specialist (P.P.S.) and still do workshops on personal and home security.

This background allowed me the opportunity to deal with a wide variety of situations and people. I have handled VIP protection, assaults, thefts, fires and much more. Does this mean that I know all there is to know about personal security? Not even close. However, I do happen to know more about the subject than the average person and that experience is what I am going to try to convey to you.

One of the most important aspects of improving your security is coming to grips with the fact that in order to be more secure in your life is that you will have to be inconvenienced. What I am talking about here is changes in your routines and way of thinking in regards to how you protect yourself. Being inconvenienced is not something that people handle well. We like order and routine as part of our life; it makes us feel more comfortable and less stressed. The down side is that familiarity breeds contempt.

What am I talking about in regards to being inconvenienced? It means making changes in your routines. Making sure you are walking and driving around with a higher degree of awareness to your surroundings. Looking at people and situations with a more objective perspective. Why has that car been cruising the neighborhood for the last two days? It's July but the guy who just walked into the store has on a full length coat. That graffiti on the fence wasn't there on Friday. These are of course only a minimal example of what I am talking about. You have to learn to see, not just look.

What follows next is a copy of the Security Survey I wrote up some time back and modified as needed. It is what

I use to survey locations to better judge their vulnerabilities so those areas can addressed. First you will see the list, then I will take each question in turn and break it down so you can better understand the reasoning behind it. So please go ahead and read the survey now.

SECURITY / SAFETY SURVEY

House

- HOW FAR BACK FROM THE STREET IS THE HOME?
- ARE THERE ANY STREET LIGHTS NEAR THE HOME?
  - IF YES, DO THEY LIGHT AN ACCEPTABLE LEVEL OF THE PROPERTY?
  - DOES ANYTHING BLOCK THE VIEW OF THE WINDOWS / DOOR?
- IS THE GARAGE CONNECTED TO THE HOME?
- IS THERE AN INTERIOR DOOR TO THE HOME? SOLID CORE?
- IF YES, DOES THE DOOR HAVE A DEADBOLT LOCK?
- IS THE FRONT DOOR A SOLID CORE DOOR?
- DOES THE FRONT DOOR HAVE A DEADBOLT LOCK?
- IF YES, DOUBLE KEY OR THUMB LOCK?

- IF THE FRONT DOOR HAS WINDOWS AND THEY ARE BROKEN CAN SOMEONE REACH IN AND REACH THE INSIDE RELEASE FOR THE DEADBOLT?

- DOES THE REAR DOOR HAVE A DEADBOLT LOCK?

- IF YES, DOUBLE KEY OR THUMB LOCK?

- DO THE FIRST FLOOR WINDOWS HAVE LOCKS?

- IS THERE AN ALARM SYSTEM?

- IF YES, WHAT TYPE OF SENSORS?

- IS THE SYSTEM EXTERNALLY MONITORED?

- IS THERE A CCTV SYSTEM IN PLACE AND BEING USED?

- IF YES, HOW MANY CAMERAS AND WHAT TYPE?

- IF YES, DOES THE SYSTEM HAVE RECORD CAPABILITY?

- IS THE RECORD CAPABILITY TAPE, CD-ROM, OR DIGITAL?

- DOES THE HOME HAVE SMOKE DETECTORS?

- IF YES, ONE IN EACH BEDROOM, KITCHEN AND HALLWAY(S)?

- DOES THE HOME HAVE A CO_2 DETECTOR?

- DOES THE HOME HAVE A CURRENT FIRE EXTINGUISHER?

EXTERIOR AREAS

- HOW FAR TO THE NEAREST RESIDENCE?

- IS THERE A FENCE? IF YES WHAT TYPE, HOW TALL?

- IS THE DRIVEWAY GATED?

- ARE THERE EXTERIOR LIGHTS? MANUAL OR MOTION?

- ARE THE LIGHTS HIGH ENOUGH TO AVOID TAMPERING?

- ARE THERE ANY DARK SPACES?

- COULD SOMEONE HIDE BETWEEN THE HOUSE AND LANDSCAPING?

MISCELLANEOUS

- IS THERE AN ACTIVE NEIGHBORHOOD WATCH PROGRAM?

-o-

Some of the questions might have made you wonder why I have them on the list. Let's take a look at each question in turn.

HOW FAR BACK FROM THE STREET IS THE HOME? – This gives you the chance to judge how much lighting will be needed to provide coverage especially if the home is further back from the street/road.

ARE THERE ANY STREET LIGHTS NEAR THE

HOME? – Criminals love it when it is dark out. Lighting is one of the most effective and least expensive security measures you can employ. Darkness works for them and against you.

IF YES, DO THEY LIGHT AN ACCEPTABLE LEVEL OF THE PROPERTY? – The light only does its job if it is used properly. Does it mean you have to illuminate the entire property? No, of course not. But the area around the front, back/side doors, around the garage and if possible near the windows, should all be lit.

DOES ANYTHING BLOCK THE VIEW OF THE WINDOWS/DOOR? – Any chance of something blocking your view in and out? Something large enough for someone to hide behind could provide cover so they could surprise you as are coming in or out.

IS THE GARAGE CONNECTED TO THE HOME? – Someone coming home using a remote garage door opener without paying attention to the area could allow a hidden assailant to slip unseen into the garage while the driver is focused on properly parking. Once the garage door is closed the assailant then surprises the driver who is now no longer visible to anyone outside.

IS THERE AN INTERIOR DOOR TO THE HOME? SOLID CORE? – The door leading into the house from the garage should be locked when someone leaves, it should be locked at night as well. If someone gains access to the garage as above, they may get in when you are leaving with the intent of robbing the house. A sturdy door with a good heavy lock might be sufficient to keep an intruder out of the house.

IF YES, DOES THE DOOR HAVE A DEADBOLT LOCK? – For the reason we just discussed in the last item.

IS THE FRONT DOOR A SOLID CORE DOOR? – This is an absolute must for the front door. It may not prevent someone from battering down the door but it won't be quiet and it won't be as easy.

DOES THE FRONT DOOR HAVE A DEADBOLT LOCK? – In the overwhelming majority of cases this is the most used access point into the home. You need to be able to secure this door as strongly as possible.

IF YES, DOUBLE KEY OR THUMB LOCK? – A double keyed lock means that it is much harder for someone to trip the lock from the inside to gain access such as reaching through broken glass panels.

IF THE FRONT DOOR HAS WINDOWS AND THEY ARE BROKEN CAN SOMEONE REACH IN AND REACH THE INSIDE RELEASE FOR THE DEADBOLT? – This is a tried and true method for some burglars. If the front door has windows of some kind make sure they are far enough away from the doorknob and locks on the inside of the door.

DOES THE REAR DOOR HAVE A DEADBOLT LOCK? - This can be easily overlooked since many homes have a fence around the back yard with gates so it is wrongly assumed that it is less likely to be targeted. In fact it is the opposite. Back doors are often targeted because the yard is fenced. The fence keeps the intruder hidden from the view of neighbors. Having a secure front AND back door is important.

IF YES, DOUBLE KEY OR THUMB LOCK? – Just as above a double keyed lock means that it is much harder for someone to trip the lock from the inside to gain access such as reaching through broken glass panels.

DO THE FIRST FLOOR WINDOWS HAVE LOCKS? – I am talking about making sure that you control the amount of movement the window is capable of making. This means both vertically and horizontally depending upon the type of window. Commercial locks are available at hardware stores at very reasonable prices.

IS THERE AN ALARM SYSTEM? – Prices for alarm systems have fallen steadily since quality systems came onto the market. Today's systems will not only alert for improper entrance but can have additional sensors added to alert in case of fire as well.

IF YES WHAT TYPE OF SENSORS? – In many cases you have a mix of sensors such motion detection, smoke and even Carbon Monoxide which further protects you and your family.

IS THE SYSTEM EXTERNALLY MONITORED? - Having an alarm system is a good idea but it is only as good as the person being aware of an alarm if it's activated. If your system is monitored by someone in a remote location (a security service, for example) then it means someone is watching your home at all times when the system is armed.

IS THERE A CCTV SYSTEM IN PLACE AND BEING USED? – The cost of a quality multi-camera system is still a bit high for most buyer's tastes. However a few facts to consider: A color camera allows you to observe areas you cannot see from inside the house; it is also possible that having the system will lower your homeowners insurance premium some. If so then the system begins paying for itself.

IF YES, HOW MANY CAMERAS AND WHAT TYPE? – You will have the choice between color and black/white, as well as infrared for night viewing. Many systems also incorporate sound into their cameras as well meaning that you would have the option of being able to remotely listen in what is going on outside. Most of the packaged systems available today come with four cameras. I am of the opinion that more is better.

IF YES, DOES THE SYSTEM HAVE RECORD CAPABILITY? – This is a very important feature of the system. If some type of illegal activity is captured by the system the recording might be the only proof of it. In this case a video is worth a thousand words. Pretty hard for a criminal to dispute solid video evidence.

IS THE RECORD CAPABILITY TAPE, CD-ROM OR DIGITAL? – Of the three choices digital is far the best. No need to change out the media device which means you can be away from home for extended periods without worry about losing the recording capability.

DOES THE HOME HAVE SMOKE DETECTORS? – This isn't necessarily a security item but it is very important to help safeguard your family. There should one in each bedroom, above the stairs (if applicable) in the kitchen and hallway. The batteries should be changed twice a year to

ensure proper operations. Swap the batteries out at change to and from Daylight Saving Time.

DOES THE HOME HAVE A CO2 DETECTOR? – Carbon Monoxide is colorless and odorless making it impossible for a person to smell or see. CO2 detectors are very reasonably priced and a worthwhile investment.

DOES THE HOME HAVE A CURRENT FIRE EXTINGUISHER? – Every home should have at least one, more is better! The best choice is an ABC style unit which works on ordinary combustibles, flammable liquids and energized electrical equipment. A quality three pound extinguisher is very reasonably priced and widely available.

HOW FAR TO THE NEAREST RESIDENCE? – This answer is similar to the first one on the survey. Another reason for this question is that it helps you to determine what danger fire might pose to your structure if the neighbor's house is burning. Also nice to know how far away potential help might be if there is a problem at your house.

IS THERE A FENCE? IF YES WHAT TYPE, HOW TALL? – A fence can serve multiple purposes. It defines the edge of your property, it can create privacy (also blind spots from street viewing so it works for and against you at times), it helps safeguard your children by keeping them in a contained area and if you have a pool out of the water (make sure if you have a pool that the fence has a locking gate as well). The type of fence determines how secure your area is. If it is just a decorative split rail fence it provides no real security. A chain link fence works well in that but isn't that aesthetically pleasing. A high wooden fence works well in both categories. How tall a fence is also is a factor in determining how secure an area might be. An experienced criminal can scale a six foot fence in little time but a few feet higher and the job takes them much longer.

IS THE DRIVEWAY GATED? – One of the keys to proper area security is ensuring that you are the one controlling as much of the access to the property as possible. If you have a fence around the yard but no gate then it somewhat defeats the purpose of the fence. One note about gates, if your gate has a powered opener what is your plan to open/close the gate in case of a power outage?

ARE THERE EXTERIOR LIGHTS? MANUAL OR MOTION? – As we discussed above lighting is a very useful and inexpensive means of deterrence. Having proper exterior lighting is very important. Having a combination of motion activated lights and manually controlled units will usually provide the best coverage. When setting up the motion activated lights make sure that the sensitivity setting is properly adjusted. If the lights come on at the slightest hint of motion then you will because desensitized to them and complacent.

ARE THE LIGHTS HIGH ENOUGH TO AVOID TAMPERING? - Have the lights mounted high enough that someone on the ground cannot simply reach up and unscrew the bulbs.

ARE THERE ANY DARK SPACES? – Once it is fully dark outside turn on all the outside lights then walk around the house to see if there are any areas that are not illuminated well enough that someone could hide in.

COULD SOMEONE HIDE BETWEEN THE HOUSE AND LANDSCAPING? – I have dealt with this circumstance several times on surveys. People invest large amounts of time, energy and money in creating beautiful hedges and other landscaping features around their homes. At the same time they are creating perfect hiding places for criminals. Make sure that there is no way someone could be lurking in between the bushes and home.

IS THERE AN ACTIVE NEIGHBORHOOD WATCH PROGRAM? – This can be a useful program to help counter-act crime in some areas but it takes the active participation of a number of people. One important note about a Watch program, once it begins it may seem that crime is actually rising but that isn't true. It is at the same level it was before but now it is getting noticed. A Watch program can be a useful vehicle to get people to get to know their neighbors. Ask yourself, how often do you speak to your neighbors? Do you know all their names, the names of their children? Speak with the Police or Sheriff's Department if you want help with getting a Watch program started in your area.

-o-

What are some of the other things that you can do to better safeguard you and your family? Glad you asked. Let's take a look at some ideas:

Don't put your child's name on the back of their shoes or buy name plates for their bicycles. This can give child predators an easy way to establish contact with your child. "Hi Sally, how are you? Can you help me? I lost my puppy, would you help me look for it?" As a parent myself I know it's a frightening thought but I promise you that there are those out that are evil enough to hurt children.

Have a safe word set up for you and your child(ren). This prevents a stranger from being able to fool them into getting into a vehicle. "Hi, I'm a friend of your Dad's and he asked me to come get you and bring you home today." Teach your child to ask, "What's the safe word?" If the person doesn't know the safe word, tell the child to run away, not walk, *run*. Practice this like a game until the child understands the rules.

Make sure that the school has a current phone number and address for those who do have permission to pick up your kids.

Many Police Departments offer fingerprinting for children as well as I.D. style cards.

Get into a routine of checking the doors and windows before turning in at night. It would also not be unwise to keep at least the door knob locked on the front door when you are home. That is a tactic used by some home invaders, they simply walk up and try the door. If it is unlocked they enter and rob the family.

Security is about creating layers of protection around you.

In conclusion....

I want to make this point very, very clear. Despite what many salesmen would have you believe, there is NO one product or technique that will guarantee your safety. It just isn't true. It takes a combination of awareness, techniques and products to better increase the odds of your safety and security. If you flash a wad of cash all the time, someone will see it. If you have a habit of tossing out your bank statements and other personal information into the trash without shredding it someone will find it, if you are not careful keeping your home secure you greatly increase the chances that you will targeted.

Stay smart and stay safer.

-o-

NOTES

GLOSSARY

2 WD – When the drive-train of a vehicle applies power to only one set of wheels. Could be either front or back wheels.

4 WD – When the drive-train of a vehicle applies power to both sets of wheels. In some vehicles this is known as all-wheel drive. In off road vehicle the application of 4WD may be done manually as needed.

A.B.C. – Airway, Breathing, Circulation. A quick and easy way to remember basic medical patient assessment. You check their Airway to make sure it is clear, see if they are Breathing and if they have a heartbeat (Circulation) or if any bleeding if present.

Abdominal Thrust – Another term for the Heimlich Maneuver which is used to help dislodge an object stuck in the airway of a choking victim.

Abrasion – an injury that rubs or scrapes away surface tissue.

A.C. – Alternating Current. The kind of electricity that is in your home.

Acute – defines the sudden onset, usually within 12 hours of an illness.

A.E.D. – Automated External Defibrillator. A portable electrical device that can be used to deliver a precise electrical shock to stabilize irregular heartbeats or to stimulate the heart muscle into beating.

Aerosol – Small particles suspended in air or other gas. Some chemical and biological weapons can be delivered in this fashion making them even more easily spread.

A.I.D.S. – Acquired Immune Deficiency Syndrome. A serious disease of the body's immune system.

Airborne Transmission – The spread of disease causing particles through the air.

Air Splint – A plastic inflatable splint used to immobilize an arm or leg suspected of being broken. These can also be used to control bleeding.

Airway – The passage for air into the body. Compromise of this airway can lead to immediate, serious health issues such as unconsciousness and death.

Airway Obstruction – Anything that completely or partially blocks the passage of air in the airway.

AK-47 – One of the most widely produced weapons ever. Originally developed by Alexander Kalashnikov in the 1940's it and its many variants become the standard weapons for the former Warsaw Pact nations and their client states. Uses a 7.62 x 39 mm cartridge. An accurate and reliable weapon.

Alpha Radiation – one of the three types of radiation emitted by nuclear weapons. Alpha is the least hazardous of the three and can be blocked by clothing.

A.L.I.C.E. – All purpose, Lightweight, Individual, Carrying, Equipment. The name for a large military back pack that is well suited for preparedness as well.

ALS – Advanced Life Support. This is medical care above and beyond that of initial Basic care.

Altered State of Consciousness – This is a serious condition and should be treated as such. It may be caused by drugs, alcohol, trauma or mental illness.

A.M. – Amplitude Modulation. The range of frequencies between 118 and 136 mHz. This is the AM side of your radio dial.

American Red Cross – A national organization dedicated to disaster response, CPR and emergency health care training.

Anaphylactic Shock – This is a very serious medical condition that occurs when the body is exposed to substance that it is allergic to such as bee venom or seafood. Death can result as a response to this condition.

AR-15 – The civilian version of the U.S. Military's standard Main Battle Rifle (MBR) the M-16. It is chambered in .223 also known as 5.56 mm. It is a gas operated, shoulder fired, air cooled, magazine fed rifle.

Antibiotic – The substance with the ability to kill or prevent the growth of a living organism such as bacteria.

Antiseptic – A substance, technique or method of treatment that is used to stop the growth of microorganisms.

Artery – The largest of the three types of blood vessels in the body, carries blood away from the heart.

Assessment – This is a medical term for determining the status of a patient. This includes but is not limited to ensuring viable airway, amount of bleeding, fractures and mental state.

A.W.D. – All Wheel Drive. Several commercially available vehicles are equipped with this style of drive wheels.

Azimuth –This is a bearing or direction. Used in navigation.

B.T.U. – (British Thermal Unit) This is the amount of energy it requires to raise the temperature of one pound of water from 39 to 40 degrees Fahrenheit.

Bacteria – These are one-celled microorganisms that can cause infection.

Bandage – This refers to a covering of gauze or other material used to apply pressure, hold dressings in place over wounds, immobilize or in some way support.

Barrel – The tube like section of a firearm through which the bullet passes after being fired.

Biological Agent – This is a toxic or infectious agent that may used against living targets. It is estimated that more than 1,200 different types of biological agents exist in the world.

Body Armor – Protective garments that are often erroneously referred to as "bullet proof vests". These come in a variety of protection levels and usually made of synthetic material. Some of these garments come with metal or ceramic inserts to further improve protection.

Botulism – An often fatal form of food poisoning which can come about from eating improperly cooked or canned foods. This is a very serious illness.

Blood Agent - A chemical compound that interferes with the oxygen carry capability of the blood.

Body Fluid Isolation – Once known as Universal Precautions this is the careful and constant creation of barriers to keep foreign fluids from coming in contact with your own skin greatly reducing the risk of exposure to disease. This is accomplished by wearing proper gloves, eye protection and when appropriate disposable outer garments.

Bolt – This is part of a rifle or shotgun which moves as part of the working action of the weapon. In many firearms the firing pin is contained within the bolt. The bolt can be manually moved to either place a cartridge in position to be fired or when pulled to the rear extract the fired casing from the weapon.

Brown Out – When electrical power demands are greater than the supply service areas may experience a dimming of lights and reduced capability of electrical appliances.

Bullet – The projectile part of a firearm cartridge.

Burn – An injury to tissue from heat, radiation or chemical exposure. A serious burn can be life threatening.

C.B. – Citizens Band Radio. Hugely popular in the 1970's and a still considered a decent means of communications.

C.C.T.V. – Closed Circuit Tele-Vision. Security systems are the most well known form of CCTV. Used in a wide variety of security applications such are casinos and retail stores.

C.C.W. – Carrying Concealed Weapon. A license issued by the appropriate agency allowing an individual to wear a firearm in a manner that obscures it from casual view. There are some states that do no allow a CCW to be carried at all. Also know as a CWP.

Clip – A retainer device to hold cartridges for use in pistols. Often fits within the pistol.

COMSEC – An acronym for Communications Security.

Cord – Used to describe an amount of wood usually firewood. It measures 4 x 4 x 8 feet totaling 128 cubic feet.

C.P.R. – Cardio-Pulmonary Resuscitation. A means of artificially continuing respirations and circulation in a person. It is a combination of external chest compressions and mouth to mouth breathing. It is recommended that everyone be certified in CPR. Classes are available through the American Red Cross, American Heart Association and local hospitals.

Capillary – One of the three types of blood vessels found in the body. These are the small size vessels.

Cartridge – The proper term for a complete unit of firearm ammunition. It consists of a bullet, a casing, a primer and the powder.

Casing – The part of a firearm cartridge that holds the powder, primer and until fired the bullet.

Charge Controller – An electronic device used to control the flow of electricity from an alternative power source, usually solar panels, to storage batteries. It is an important part of an alternative energy system as it helps to limit any damage to the batteries.

Chemical Agent – Toxic chemical compounds used for crowd control or to incapacitate. The most common examples of this are riot control agents.

Cylinder – The circular section of a revolver that holds the cartridges and rotates them into position to be fired. This rotating action is how the revolver got its name. Depending upon the caliber the cylinder may hold as few as two cartridges or as many as nine.

Direct Current – Electrical current of constant magnitude that flows in only one direction.

Direct Pressure – This is usually the most reliable way to stop bleeding. Holding a dressing atop the wound and applying steady pressure to slow and hopefully stop the bleeding.

D.F. – Direction Finding. A means of electronically determining the direction from where a radio signal was transmitted from.

Dressing – This is a covering for a wound that is held in place by a bandage.

Emergency – An unexpected situation that occurs suddenly which has the potential to cause injuries and/or damage property.

EMS – Emergency Medical System – A comprehensive treatment system for the care of ill and injured persons involving both pre-hospital and hospital care.

E.M.T. – Emergency Medical Technician. A person trained to respond to pre-hospital medical conditions and give care sufficient to allow the patient to be transported to a medical facility.

Endemic – Disease or illness common to a particular area or population.

Epidemic – A disease that occurs beyond the boundaries of a normal outbreak in a specific area or population.

Event – An incident that disrupts normal activities and has the potential for injury and property damage.

Fallout – The spread of radioactive waste products after the release of radioisotopes such as a nuclear blast or accidental discharge from a nuclear power plant. Fallout may be measured using a detection meter.

Faraday Cage – An enclosure of some type that will help shield the contents from external static electrical fields.

FEMA – Federal Emergency Management Agency. A division of the Department of Homeland Security charged with responding to disasters on a federal level.

FFL – Federal Firearms License. This is a license issued by the Bureau of Alcohol, Tobacco and Firearms (BATF) which allows a business or individual to be able to legally manufacture and / or sell firearms and ammunition.

FIFO – First In First Out. A method of storage in which the older goods are placed toward the front of the storage unit to ensure that they are used up prior to the newer goods.

First Aid – The initial medical response to an illness or injury. This can often be given by non medically trained individuals prior to the arrival of better trained and equipped personnel.

First Responder – A person with medical training less than that of an E.M.T.

Flammable – A substance that is easily ignited and capable of rapidly burning.

Frame – The body of a handgun. Similar to the chassis of a motor vehicle, this is the structure to which all the remaining parts are attached to.

FTF – Face To Face – A slang term common among those in preparedness referring to a personal meeting of at least two people.

Germ – A microorganism capable of causing disease.

Golden Horde – Refers to those people that are involved in the rapid and disorganized exodus from urban areas following some type of disaster.

Gray – A unit of measurement of the intensity of ionizing radiation that is equivalent to 100 Rads or 1 Joule per kilogram of tissue.

Grid – An outline of numbered or lettered squares placed atop a map to assist in determining locations. Also a slang reference to a regional electricity supply system.

H2H – Human To Human. The worst case scenario for the spread of a disease. This contact may be through touch or respiratory exhaust which is then breathed in by the people nearby.

Hammer – The part of a firearm which strikes the firing pin providing the force to ignite the primer causing the cartridge to fire.

Hazard – A condition that poses the risk of danger, damage and or injury.

HEPA – High Efficiency Particulate Air. Used in environments that require a higher level of air filtration such as in medical and certain manufacturing environments. True HEPA filers must trap no less than 99.97% of particles of .03 microns.

HF – High Frequency. This refers to a range of radio frequencies between 3 and 30 megahertz (MHz).

ICU – Intensive Care Unit. An area of a hospital where the most seriously injured patients are kept for treatment.

IED – Improvised Explosive Device. Most commonly known from their use during the Iraqi war by unconventional forces. It is a bomb built and deployed in a non-conventional means. They may be triggered by a cellular phone call, pressure switch, trip wire and more. These are very dangerous.

Immediate Action – A shooting term used to describe the steps to clear a firearm following a stoppage.

Infection – The invasion of the body by rapidly reproducing germs that leads to illness

Injury – Damage or harm to a person or property.

Inverter – An electrical appliance that converts DC into AC for use with common tools and appliances. They come is a variety of sizes and capabilities with many units priced well under $200.

IR – Infra-Red. A form of electromagnetic radiation. It is widely used for both military and civilian applications including night vision, remote temperature sensing and weather forecasting.

IV – Intra-Venous. A system to artificially provide fluid transfer to the body's circulatory system as well as the administration of medications

Junk Silver – U.S. coins (not nickels or pennies) that were made prior to 1965 which are made primarily from high content silver. Starting in 1965 the metal content of these coins were changed.

KI – Potassium Iodine. Most widely known in the preparedness community as a means of protecting the thyroid gland from certain types of radiation exposure. Available in pill form.

K.I.S.S. – Keep It Simple Stupid. Speaks for itself.

KHz – KiloHertz. A measurement of frequency equal to 1,000 hertz and is used to help measure alternating current and audio signals.

KT – Kilo Ton. An amount equal to 1,000 metric tons. Often used to describe the blast capability of large scale weapons such as atomic or nuclear warheads.

LBE – Load Bearing Equipment. Also known as LBE, this is strap or vest system used to hold and transport a wide variety of equipment and supplies.

LEO – Law Enforcement Officer

Magazine – A container that holds firearms cartridges.

Medevac – A word formed from the term Medical Evacuation which is used to describe a system of patient transport to a facility where a higher level of treatment is available.

M.O.P.P. – Mission Orientated Protective Posture – A U.S. military term for garments worn to protect the wearer from the affects of a selection of Nuclear, Biological or Chemical weapons.

MRE – Meals Ready to Eat. A bagged meal consisting of an entrée, side dishes, drink mix and dessert. These were created for the U.S. military but are available to civilians as well. The meals are high in calories and nutrients. The pouch is plastic and sealed to prevent water damage to the food.

MT – Mega Ton An amount equal to 1,000,000 metric tons. Often used to describe the blast capability of large scale weapons such as atomic or nuclear warheads.

Muzzle – The end of a firearm barrel from which the bullet / projectile leaves the weapon.

Muzzle Blast – The cloud of heated gas and spent powder that exits the barrel immediately following the bullet.

N.B.C. – An acronym meaning Nuclear – Biological –

Chemical. The big three of Weapons of Mass Destruction.

Nerve Agent – A gas or liquid that affects the body's ability to transmit commands along the nerve network.

OC – Oleoresin Capsicum. A mixture of oil and resin found in nature. Used in personal defense sprays and by law enforcement.

Off Grid – Living in such a way that your power and other services are self supported.

OPSEC – An acronym for Operational Security

Pandemic – A disease that occurs throughout a population such as 1918 Spanish Flu outbreak.

Paramedic – A highly trained medical responder tasked with providing pre-hospital care. The training and certification is higher than that of an E.M.T.

Primer – The section of a firearm cartridge used to ignite the powder so that the bullet can be launched.

Powder – The propellant part of a firearm cartridge.

Pocket Dosimeter – A small device carried or worn by a person to monitor their exposure to radiation.

PVC – Poly Vinyl Chloride material used to make a wide variety of fittings, tubes and pipes. Much of a modern household plumbing system is put together using PVC pipe.

Quarantine – To isolate people affected with a communicable disease or at risk of spreading such a disease to prevent the spread of the illness.

Radiation – A byproduct of nuclear decomposition, the giving off of energy.

Safety – A mechanical means to prevent a firearm from discharging.

Sheeple – A slang term coined from the combination of the words sheep and people. Used to describe those in society who refuse to think or act for themselves.

Slide – On a semi-automatic pistol this is the upper portion of the weapon which contains the barrel. When the weapon is fired the slide travels to the rear which pulls the empty casing and ejects it. Then when traveling forward again it strips the next cartridge from the magazine and seats it in position to be fired.

Sphygmomanometer – The instrument used to measure a person's blood pressure. Also known as a BP cuff.

Stock – Similar in function to a frame in a handgun. This piece supports the other moving parts of a rifle or shotgun.

Stoppage – A shooting term used to describe a situation in which the shooter has every expectation that the firearm will discharge but doesn't.

Ten Codes – A series of radio call signs to convey specific information in a shorter period of time.

Toxic – Something that is deadly or harmful such as numerous chemical compounds.

Toxicity – How toxic a substance is.

Toxin – A substance that is poisonous.

Trauma – Physical injury as a result of violent or disruptive action.

Triage – A method in emergency medicine for determining which patients are at the greatest need and assigning them to appropriate levels of care

Trigger – The mechanical feature that is used to initiate the firing of a gun.

UHF – Ultra High Frequency

Vein – The blood vessels which returns blood to the heart to be pumped out again via arteries.

VHF – Very High Frequency. Radio frequencies between a range of 300 and 3000 megahertz (MHz).

WMD – Weapons of Mass Destruction. These are a select group of weapons capable of causing very large amounts of damage and/or casualties when deployed. Typically these refer to a nuclear device, biological or chemical agents.

Wound – Another word for injury.

WTSHTF – When The Stuff Hits The Fan – An acronym often used to describe a major event or change in one's lifestyle.

MARK A. SMITH

NOTES

PHONETIC ALPHABETS

Military - Civilian

A – ALPHA	A – ADAM
B – BRAVO	B – BOY
C - CHARLIE	C - CHARLES
D – DELTA	D – DAVID
E – ECHO	E – EDWARD
F – FOXTROT	F- FRANK
G – GOLF	G – GEORGE
H – HOTEL	H – HENRY
I – INDIA	I – IDA
J – JULIET	J - JOHN
K – KILO	K – KING
L – LIMA	L – LINCOLN
M – MIKE	M – MARY
N – NOVEMBER	N - NORA
O - OSCAR	O – OCEAN

P – PAPA	P - PAUL
Q – QUEBEC	Q – QUEEN
R – ROMEO	R – ROBERT
S – SIERRA	S – SAM
T – TANGO	T – TOM
U – UNIFORM	U -- UNION
V – VICTOR	V - VICTOR
W – WHISKEY	W - WILLIAM
X – X RAY	X – X RAY
Y- YANKEE	Y – YOUNG
Z – ZULU	Z – ZEBRA

10 CODES FOR RADIO COMMUNICATION

Keep in mind that each locality has its own codes and these may not be ones utilized by your regional authorities.

10-0 Use Caution	10-51 Wrecker Needed
10-1 Signal Weak	10-52 Ambulance Needed
10-2 Signal Good	10-53 Traffic Control
10-3 Stop Transmitting	10-54 Change to Channel #
10-4 OK, Affirmative	10-55 Intoxicated Driver
10-5 Relay to	10-56 Intoxicated Pedestrian
10-6 Busy unless Urgent	10-57 Hit and Run (F, PI, PD)
10-7 Out of Service	10-58 Airplane Crash
10-8 In Service	10-59 Reckless Driver
10-9 Say Again	10-60 Out of Car on

(Repeat)	Violator at (location)
10-10 Negative	10-61 VIN Inspection
10-11 (Person) On Duty	10-62 Request Permission Car to Car
10-12 Stand By (Stop)	10-63 Prepare to Make Written Copy
10-13 Weather Conditions	10-64 Vandalism
10-14 Message/Information	10-65 Juvenile Problem
10-15 Message Delivered	10-66 Major Crime Alert
10-16 Reply to Message	10-67 Net Message
10-17 Enroute to (location)	10-68 Runaway Juvenile
10-18 Urgent	10-69 Missing Person
10-19 (In) Contact	10-70 Fire Alarm
10-20	10-71 Nature of Fire

Location		
10-21 Call (person) by Phone		10-72 Fire Progress Report
10-22 Disregard		10-73 Rape
10-23 Arrived at Scene		10-74 Civil Disturbance
10-24 Assignment Completed		10-75 Domestic Problem
10-25 Meet with (person)		10-76 Meet Complainant
10-26 E.T.A.		10-77 Return to (Location)
10-27 DL Check		10-78 Back up (unit)
10-28 Registration Check		10-79 Notify Coroner
10-29 NCIC Check		10-80 Chase in Progress
10-30 Danger/Caution		10-81 Breathalyzer
10-31 Pick up (person)		10-82 Prisoner in Custody

10-32 (#) Units Needed	10-83 Confidential Information
10-33 Help me Quick!	10-84 Visitor Present
10-34 Current Time	10-85 Victim(s) Condition
10-35 Interdiction	A - Fair
10-36 Security Check	B - Poor
10-37 Gang Activity	C - Critical
10-38 Computer Down	D - Possible Fatality
10-39 Urgent (lights and siren)	E - Obvious Fatality
10-40 Silent Run (no lights)	10-86 Crime in Progress
10-41 Begin Tour of Duty	10-87 Abandoned Vehicle
10-42 End Tour of Duty	10-88 Man with a Gun
10-43 Shuttle	10-89 Bomb Threat

10-44 Permission to Leave	10-90 Bank Alarm at (location)
10-45 Animal Carcass at	10-91 Burglary
10-46 Assist Motorist	10-92 Theft
10-47 Investigate Vehicle	10-93 Unnecessary use of Radio
10-48 Disturbing the Peace	10-94 Contact your Home
10-49 Traffic Light Out	10-95 Out at Home
10-50 Traffic Accident	10-96 Mental Subject
(F, PI, PD)	10-97 Test Signal
	10-98 Prison Break

MARK A. SMITH

NOTES

MARK A. SMITH

NOTES

RESOURCES AND ADDITIONAL INFORMATION

Preparedness Groups

www.alpharubicon.com

www. mrssurvival.com

www.timebomb2000.com

www.frugalsquirrel.com

www.whenshtf.com

www.survivalboards.com

www.thetreeofliberty.com

www.ar15.com

Preparedness information

www.ready.gov

www.arc.com

www.backwoodshome.com

www.alpharubicon.com

Other Preparedness Information Sites

www.truthistreason.net

www.survivalblog.com

Bulk Food and Equipment Retailers

www.homespunenvironmental.com–Water filtration products

www.pantryparatus.com–Kitchen supplies of all types

www.pantryprepper.com–Thrive long term storage foods

www.beprepared.com–Food, equipment, books

www.mredepot.com–Food, equipment, supplies

www.nitropak.com–Food, equipment, books

www.waltonfeed.com–Food, seeds

www.lehmans.com–Non electric appliances, kitchen equipment, laundry equipment

www.utahsheltersystem.com–In ground shelters

www.wavecatcher.us–Shortwave radio supplies and information

Recommended Reading

Where there is no Doctor – David Werner, Carol Thurman and Jane Maxwell

Where there is no Dentist – Murray Dickson

The Encyclopedia of Country Living – Carla Emery

Life after Doomsday – Bruce Clayton

Life after Terrorism – Bruce Clayton

In the Gravest Extreme: The role of the firearms in personal protection – Massad Ayoob

Backwoods Home Magazine – A terrific magazine

FIRST AID KIT SUPPLIES

Trauma Supplies

30 Individual packages of sterile 4x4's (Minimum)
20 Individual packages of sterile 2x2's   (Minimum)
10 sterile oval eye patches
20 rolls of gauze bandage
5 chemical ice packs
5 chemical heat packs
4 four inch ACE wraps
4 three inch ACE wraps
4 ladder or SAM splints
2 pairs of Trauma Shears
2-4 boxes of unsterile gloves
2 Penlights
5 Bottles of Isopropyl Alcohol
5 Bottles of Hydrogen Peroxide
6 triangular bandages
10 rolls of Transpore or other medical tape
10 bottles of irrigation fluid (saline or sterile water)
Several boxes of assorted Band-Aids (different sizes and configurations)
10 ABD type dressings (maxi-pads work nicely!)
One tube (approximately 100) unsterile 4x4 dressings
One tube (approximately 100) unsterile 2x2 dressings

Medications

2 bottles of Ibuprofen	2 bottles of Acetaminophen
2 bottles of Aspirin	2 bottles of Antacid
2 Bottles of Benadryl	2 Bottles decongestant (Sudafed)

4 Bottles of cough medicine	5 bags of cough drops
2 Bottles of Nyquil	4 Bottles of Calamine Lotion
Several Sting-Eze Swabs	4 Cans of SolarCaine Spray
5 tubes of Antibiotic ointment	5 tubes of hydrocortisone ointment
2 tubes of hemorrhoid cream	Children's strength medications
4 Tubes of InstaGlucose	4 Bottles of Bactine or astringent
2 Bottles of Syrup of Ipecac	2 Boxes of Ammonia Inhalants
3 large boxes of Alcohol Prep pads	2 large bottles of betadine

3 large boxes of betadine Prep Pads
One bottle of eye wash for each person in your family

Other Supplies
Stethoscope

Blood Pressure Cuff
CPR mask with one-way valve

Vaseline or KY lubricant

Oral and Rectal Thermometers with Probe covers

SUGGESTED FOOD LIST
See Foods Chapter for listing information

Baking mixes	Baking powder
Baking soda	Barley
Bay leaves	Beans-dry
Bread crumbs	Bottled drinks / juices
Brown Sugar	Bullion
Butter flavoring	Candy
Canned beans	Canned broth
Canned chicken	Canned tomatoes/sauces
Canned French fried onions	Canned fruit
Canned pie filling	Canned pumpkin
Canned Salmon	Canned soups
Canned stews	Canned sweet potatoes
Canned Tuna	Canned veggies
Cans of lemonade mix	Canned dry drink mixes
Cheese dips	Cheese soups
Chili	Chinese food spices

Chocolate bars	Chinese ingredients
Chocolate chips	Chocolate syrup
Coffee filters	Condensed Milk
Corn Masa de Harina	Corn tortilla mix
Corn meal	Corn starch
Crackers	Cream of Wheat
Cream soups	Crisco
Dried eggs	Dried fruit
Dried onions	Dried soup mixes
Dry cocoa	Dry coffee creamer
Dry milk powder	Dry Mustard
Evaporated Milk	Flour (white and wheat)
Garlic powder	Granola bars
Hard candy	Honey
Hot chocolate mix	Instant coffee
Instant mashed potatoes	Jarred peppers
Jellies and Jams	Jerky
Ketchup	Kool Aid
Lard	Marshmallow cream

Marshmallows	Mayo packets
Mexican food ingredients	Mustard
Nestle Table Cream	Nuts
Oatmeal	Oil
Olive oil	Olives
Onion powder	Parmesan cheese
Pasta	Peanut butters
Pepper	Pet food
Pickles	Relish
Powdered sugar	Power bars
Raisins	Ramen style noodles
Ravioli	Real butter
Rice	Salsa and hot sauces
Salt	Spam or Treet
Spices and herbs	Stovetop Dressing mix
Strawberry syrup	Sugar
Summer sausage	Syrups (Pancake)
Tea bags	Trail mix

Tuna	Ultra pasteurized milk
Vanilla	Velveeta cheese
Vienna sausage	Yeast

ABOUT THE AUTHOR

Mark A. Smith brings a strong background in preparedness know-how to this book, the consequence of decades of working in the fields of safety, security, firefighting, emergency medical care, and hazardous materials handling. He has been a Preparedness Consultant since 2001. Among his background experience is a 3-year stint as Safety/Security Director at the Blue Ridge Job Corps Center, Fire Chief/Firefighter at Lackawanna Volunteer Fire Department in Ely NV, and an EMT-I at Ely Volunteer

Ambulance Services.

He did a tour with the Marines, 1982-89, and served in the Indiana National Guard (including riot control training). He has been a presenter at two national safety and health conferences, discussing hazardous materials handling and awareness, and is the author of four articles on haz-mat handling. He put his life on the line for two years as a Certified Wildland Firefighter.

Today, Mark is the owner of Southern Plains Consulting, an Oklahoma-based preparedness firm. He is active as a speaker, lecturer, and participant at multiple preparedness conferences, and has been the primary developer of three expos devoted to survival and preparations. Mark lives on a working farm, and participates in cattle handling and care, as well as crop preparation and harvesting.

He brings this wealth of knowledge and experience to this book, his second publication with Auctoritas Publishing. His first book, an alternative history novella, *Roma Victrix*, has sold internationally. It is also available on Amazon.com as a Kindle ebook.

NOTES

Made in the USA
Charleston, SC
23 October 2012